TOM JONES

A LIFE IN PICTURES

Published in 2013 by Carlton Books
An imprint of the Carlton Publishing Group
20 Mortimer Street
London W1T 3JW

A CIP catalogue record for this book is available from the British Library.

ISBN 978 1 78097 257 2

Printed in Dubai.

TOM JONES

A LIFE IN PICTURES

CHRIS ROBERTS

CARLTON

INTRODUCTION

He was 'Jones The Voice' long before TV show *The Voice* was
even a twinkle in a BBC programmer's eye. He's sung with
everyone from Elvis Presley to Van Morrison, from Robbie
Williams to Jack White. He had his first number one hit – 'It's
Not Unusual' – on March 1 (St David's Day) 1965, and his
most recent top ten album – *Spirit In The Room* – in summer
2012, 47 years later. He's sold over 100,000,000 albums
worldwide. Knighted for services to music in 2006, Sir Tom
Jones has crossed decades and genres to become and remain
one of the most popular British singers of all time, and one
of the planet's biggest stars. He's been balladeer, rocker, soul
man, R&B belter, dance act, and gospel crooner. Working
class hero, sex symbol, Vegas legend, master of knowing
reinvention, Sir Tom is, at 72 years of age, still singing and
swinging, a genuine icon in an age when the word has been
devalued. He's come a long, long way since debuting as Tiger
Tom the Twisting Vocalist.

'Tiger Tom the Twisting Vocalist' was the memorable moniker under which Tom, a coalminer's son, performed while learning his craft in the Welsh valleys' working men's clubs. Now a showbiz monolith, he struggled at first: as the Sixties (and his twenties) dawned, Tom Woodward was unknown. He had also become a young husband and father, at 17. He'd sing the living daylights out of rock'n'roll standards in front of a supportive crowd of pals who'd possibly had a drink or two, but he had no real clue how to make a career of his obvious gift.

W hen top manager of the era (and local boy made good) Gordon Mills witnessed him in action, he saw it at once. He knew that this wanton Welsh hurricane with the black man's voice and untethered pelvis was something special. The voice was sensational, all-conquering, and if the physical appeal might be considered too much, too masculine for the mop-top generation, then Tom could top the charts by wooing their mums as a way in to the charts. It was clear to Mills that no barrier would be too high for that voice, that easy libidinous charm. But those barriers put up a fight at first…

As Tom hit London as the singer of Tommy Scott and The Senators, later The Squires, he encountered resistance, and couldn't catch a break. He spent despondent, hungry nights with the band in a less than glamorous Ladbroke Grove hotel, waiting for luck to change. They made a record and it flopped, and he considered packing it in and moving back to South Wales. He was rarely if ever starved of female company, but missed Pontypridd and his wife and son. And then that seismic change of fortune came. Mills offered Sandie Shaw a song he'd co-written as a follow-up to her hit 'Always Something There To Remind Me'. She passed on it. Tom snapped it up. The song was 'It's Not Unusual', and it meant that for Tom '65 was a very good year to be alive. When the single went to number one, he was on tour with Cilla Black and Tommy Roe. He celebrated the news by drinking till dawn – a not uncommon occurrence for him then. The song rocketed him into the American top ten too, and after that he was a bona fide, charisma-fuelled superstar, a live-show attraction and a hit machine. Those hits have

RIGHT: 'Jones The Voice' – one of the planet's biggest stars.

become a part of Britain's (and especially Wales') national identity: the film themes like 'What's New Pussycat?' and 'Thunderball', the unapologetically emotive ballads such as 'The Green, Green Grass Of Home', 'Delilah', 'Till' and 'I'm Coming Home', and the licentious hip-wrigglers like 'She's A Lady' and 'Help Yourself'. The hits stopped coming for a while after the mid-Seventies, and Tom 'languished' on the well-reimbursed live circuit in the States, on the verge of self-parody. Yet he was to bounce back with a canny stylistic reboot to offer the likes of 'Kiss' and 'Sex Bomb' – and then to just keep on reloading.

His love life was always a scandal-magnet for the press. From the early breakthrough, they couldn't equate this lusty onstage mover with the fact that he was "happily married". And along the way the heart-throb's indiscretions were high-profile tabloid fodder. The marriage survives and their son has proven invaluable to his dad's career, as we shall later see.

In his first bloom Tom Jones secured his own spectacular weekly TV show in the UK, which drew the biggest names in showbiz as eager guests. He then triumphed in America, where he took top ratings on ABC. Many saw him as Elvis Presley's main rival, but the pair became good friends. Weaving between the underwear thrown at him onstage by adoring female fans, he dabbled in the movie world but found a second home in Las Vegas, where his feverishly exciting concerts more than matched the city's exuberant temperature and tone. By '74 he was hanging out with Muhammad Ali and celebrating his 34th birthday backstage with Liberace and Debbie Reynolds.

As he wowed American showbiz royalty he perhaps began to lose his hold over British audiences, and his chart performances in his homeland stuttered. He attempted a country career in Nashville, signing a long-term deal. Then mentor Gordon Mills died. As Jones swerved into his late forties (in the late Eighties), it appeared to some –

especially the new generation – that he had had his glory days and was washed up. And this is where his son, Mark Woodward, saved the day.

Mark felt the pulse of the modern music industry. He suggested Tom ditch the cheese, or at least wink and show he was aware of it. He encouraged him to pursue his authentic love of music: of rock, soul and funk. And in 1988 his cover of Prince's 'Kiss', complete with contemporary trappings, shot him back into the Top Ten. He hooked up with left-field, non-mainstream acts to emerge with the album *The Lead And How To Swing It*. From then on that new generation queued up to collaborate with Jones and bask in his reflected status. His willingness to poke fun at himself also endeared him to the new world: there was affection mixed in with the awe. From working with Wyclef Jean to covering Arctic Monkeys, from releasing minimalist blues albums to mentoring others on the aforementioned family-friendly

TV show *The Voice* (one of his charges, naturally, won it), he's continued to surprise and rise from strength to strength.

His has been an impossibly glamorous life, from buying Dean Martin's old house (and then selling it on to Nicolas Cage) to jamming with Aretha and Elvis, but audiences sense an earthiness at heart in Tom Jones, a credibility that transcends musical fashions and certainly age. He's a multi-millionaire granddad who still shows the young' uns how it's done. Sir Tom is a bomb bigger than time.

His vibrant story is long, strong and full of song.

OPPOSITE : Tom Jones then.
"A wanton Welsh hurricane with an easy libidinous charm".

ABOVE: Tom Jones now. "A multi-millionaire granddad who still shows the young 'uns how it's done".

1
FROM THE VALLEYS TO THE PEAKS

Tom was supposed to be a miner, like his father. Where he came from – a poor, working-class district – that was the normal (sometimes only) career path. Yet when he contracted tuberculosis in his teens, he was confined to bed for almost two years. It wasn't the ideal thing to happen to a young singer. He's said that when he recovered it was the happiest moment of his life.

Thomas John Woodward Senior, Tom's dad, met Freda Jones at a local dance in 1933. After marrying, they moved in with Freda's parents in the small village of Treforest, around the corner from Pontypridd in the Rhondda Valley. Their daughter Sheila was born in 1934 and son Tom – given the same full name as his father – arrived in 1940. As it tends to in Wales, the voice ran in the family.

Thomas Senior had often been acclaimed for his singing, along with his brothers George and Edwin. He and his wife later recalled young Tom making noises "like musical notes" as an infant: apparently he didn't take kindly to being interrupted. Freda claimed she always knew he had a special talent: he could sing before he could walk. Heck, he could sing before he could stand. Aged two years old, he'd hide himself behind the curtains, clear his throat (something Tom still famously does), and demand that his mother call him out onto "the stage". Tom has said he'd wriggle about happily to any upbeat song that blasted out of the radio. In the corner shop, he'd clamber up onto a box and sing to any customers who cared to pay attention. Then there were family get-togethers, where singing was compulsory – weddings, Christmas parties, his mother's Women's Guild meetings – all good practice. Sometimes, Tom would win not just applause, but pennies. His confidence high, he was to graduate to talent contests and the area's working men's club-and-pub scene.

When he was four, his family moved to a terraced house with three storeys in Laura Street, and the boy from nowhere had his own room. By his own admission (and his teachers have backed him up), he wasn't an A-student at school. He wasn't especially interested in academia. He did join the school choir (few didn't, in those parts), and was once admonished for drowning out the rest of the school in assembly, during a particularly rousing rendition of Welsh anthem 'Men Of Harlech'. Upon reaching teenage years he misbehaved, often playing truant from school. He preferred idling at the local swimming baths.

That can't have helped with the tuberculosis, which came along just after Linda had. Near-local girl Linda was born Melinda Trenchard, and for young Tom, he has always said, it was love at first sight. They didn't meet much until secondary modern, with him having attended a Protestant junior school and she a Catholic one. Tom's remembered seeing her playing marbles in the street when he was 11. Their first kiss came in a game of kiss-chase not too long afterwards. They'd canoodle on mountain tops on summer days and nights. They tied the knot on 2 March, 1957 at Pontypridd registry office, and son Mark arrived on 11 April. It wasn't odd for couples to marry young in that time and place: many of Tom's peers had started working down the mines at 15. As he himself phrased it, "Once you're working, you think you're a man. You want to go drinking with the boys. Being married is part of being an adult, of proving that you're capable."

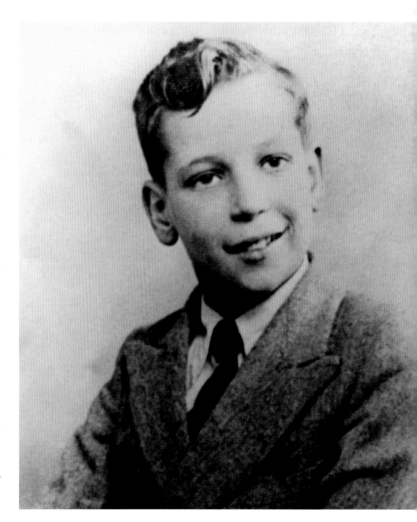

OPPOSITE: Tom's parents: Thomas John Woodward and Freda Jones.

RIGHT: Born 1940, the Tom Jones smile was there from an early age.

The tuberculosis had been a shock to the otherwise healthy lad, worrying his parents, but now everything appeared stable for the newly-weds. Little did they know how everything was to change. While laid up in bed, Tom had listened to music on the radio, soaking it up. And physically, he matured. Linda said, "When we met up again after he returned to school, I didn't recognise him at first! But I was immediately attracted to him again…" Tom was clearly enamoured, refusing to brag to boyhood friends about his sweetheart. Finding out she was pregnant was nevertheless a lot for both to deal with. Teenage pregnancy was common thereabouts in the Fifties, but still a shock. Then Tom's father asked aloud why everybody was discussing the future as if the parents-to-be had no say in the matter. "It's their life," he said, "let's hear from them." He looked over at a grateful Tom and asked him what he and Linda wanted to do. Tom instantly reasserted that the pair wanted to marry. "Go ahead," said Tom senior. They did, but not until Linda was legally of age (16) in January '57. Married in March, they moved into Linda's parents' basement. Mark was born and it dawned on Tom that he now had a family to support. And was broke. He'd previously worked as an apprentice in a glove-making factory, and not enjoyed it. He took a job working night-shifts at a paper-mill, volunteering for overtime, but still money was scarce as his youth meant he was poorly paid. When Linda went into hospital, he couldn't afford to take the night off. He learned he was a dad by ringing the hospital from a red phone box on Laura Street.

Years on, a tax exile, he bought that phone box and had it moved into the grounds of his Bel Air mansion, next to the pool. Michael Jackson admired it. But such glamour was a distance away yet. Here, he was pro-actively demanding "a man's wage" from the mill manager, and finally getting it. Trouble was, night-shifts didn't help you get booked as a singer.

"We were 16 and married with a baby, but we were happy," Tom has recalled. "We loved each other and had loving families nearby. I didn't feel all that young. In the valleys, you grow up quick."

Upon reaching 21, he quit the job, believing he could now claim a decent wage elsewhere. Relatives were very supportive while he was "on the dole", and he was singing with increasing regularity at pubs, clubs and parties. Sharp-dressed (as was his father), he started to make a bit of cash from it, gaining a reputation as a local maverick talent. From the age of 13 he'd been drinking with friends in the pubs, getting into scraps and scrapes. He was reckoned to "fancy himself", and in scenes of rough-housing his nose had been broken several times. One night he was head-butted through the glass door of the chip shop. Such moments were not atypical of growing up in South Wales. A more significant rite of passage was to come when Tom, who'd also dabbled in the guitar and in drumming, became the frontman of a local band. He had a taste, and a knack, for it.

Friday nights at the Pontypridd YMCA were a must-see. That was where young Tom Woodward threw himself into his wild-rocker persona as lead singer of The Senators, a local band with high hopes but little idea how to realise them. As step one, band leader Vernon Hopkins decided they needed to extend their name. Their previous vocalist Tommy Pittman, known onstage as Tommy Redman, had all but lost interest. (He preferred ballads to rock'n'roll. In later life he admitted he was understandably jealous when Tom made it big.) Hopkins went out to a phone box and, rifling through the pages, fancied the name Tommy Scott. So he re-titled the band Tommy Scott and The Senators. Our Tom was, for a short while, Tommy Scott.

The band had improvised through three successive Friday nights without a lead singer since the other Tommy had wandered off. Hopkins, having persuaded Tom to give his usual drinking haunt a miss by offering him a crate of beer and a share of the band's six-pounds fee, wasn't disappointed by his new protégé's performance. For his part, Tom was thrilled to be part of a group. It seemed to him then that groups were edging out solo singers, and that he needed what he looked on as a backing band. Hopkins couldn't help but recognise his talent, and after a vote was taken among the band members, Tom Woodward, or Tommy Scott, was in. The need for reliability – for turning up – was impressed upon him.

They began burning up stages, able now, with Tom's versatility, to swing between rock thumpers and hearty ballads. Tiger Tom, the Twisting Vocalist, dressed in all-black leather and became, if not quite a local celebrity, a well-known character about town. He wasn't so skint any more: added together, his Senators fees and dole money allowed him to support his wife and child and indulge in his pet hobby, heavy drinking. While the band and their very 'modern' electric guitars would warm up the crowd with instrumentals, it was not uncommon – or considered unseemly – for him to down twelve pints of bitter before taking the stage. It's been said that he might make the band (and crowd) wait a little longer if a young lady caught his eye at the bar – sometimes too long, and he tested their patience. But he always delivered and raised the temperature when the time came. Plus he was a tough guy, and it wasn't smart to tick him off. At one bar in Caerphilly, The Green Fly, he was reportedly beaten up, but when people remarked upon his cut face, he snapped, "You should see the other bloke."

As the pop music boom muscled out crooners and started taking over the Sixties, with the Beatles and Stones and beat bands in the ascendant, there was a feeling of real and quick change in the music industry. Youngsters saw their chance, dreamed of glory. Tommy and his Senators were no different:

RIGHT: Teenage sweethearts Tom and Linda married young, in March 1957.

> " *It was just a matter of time before bigger spotlights than those local papers could offer picked him out.* "

they craved fame and adulation. They didn't have the magic formula at this point, though. Tom was smart enough to take singing lessons to hone his breathing techniques, but the band lacked the fashionable fringes, the mode-ish jackets. Out of touch with the 'happening' metropolis, and far from the Mersey, they adhered to notions of cool that had been jettisoned by shifting times. They didn't write songs, and though their covers of Chuck Berry, Little Richard and Jerry Lee Lewis were given undeniable oomph by Tom's voice and sweaty confidence, they were still somehow more late Fifties than Sixties in style and attitude. For all the local fans telling Tom to go to London and make it big, South Wales wasn't yet in tune with the cutting edge. Tom himself, however, had something. He was a rough diamond. More and more, people noticed.

It was just a matter of time before bigger spotlights than those local papers could offer, picked him out. If the closest to fame Tom had previously been was chasing Jerry Lee Lewis in a taxi after the star had finished a Cardiff gig and getting his autograph, he was now to get slightly closer. He made his first tentative television appearances, singing what he admitted was "bland" material, one example being a version of 'That Lucky Old Sun' on BBC Wales' *Donald Peers Presents*. Soon the band was considered good enough to support Billy J. Kramer and the Dakotas in Porthcawl, as the headline band were topping the charts. By all accounts Tom knocked the crowd sideways and the name star said he was a tough act to follow. After two songs, Kramer realized the audience were yelling for him to "bring back Tom," and shortened his set, allowing the Senators an extended encore, just to appease the unruly mob, who gyrated along enthusiastically with the Tiger and his tank-sized voice. Still, Welsh TV and radio remained conservative compared to some areas, and worthwhile gigs that might take him to the next level were scarce. Tom, accepting he'd 'conquered' South Wales as much as anybody like him could, pondered the going-to-London idea further. Had he the courage to leave home and see if the streets were paved with record deals? He didn't know anybody there, had no contacts, and the centre of the Sixties pop universe seemed, practically, a lot further away then than now.

It was a Welshman born in the village of Tonypandy who was to be the major catalyst in Tom's metamorphosis from gifted miner's son to international sensation. Gordon Mills, once a bus conductor, had made the leap: moving to London, determined to gain a foothold in the music industry there, he'd begun as a harmonica player, then joined The Viscounts as lead vocalist. This band enjoyed a couple of minor hits, like their cover of the US hit 'Who Put The Bomp?' Gordon wanted and offered more, and wrote songs for Decca, bringing hits to Cliff Richard among others. He penned Johnny Kidd and The Pirates' 'I'll Never Get Over You'. He married a model, Jo, and when she became pregnant felt his financial future lay in song-writing, so left the band.

Meanwhile Tommy Scott and The Senators had found managers in Raymond Godfrey and John Glastonbury, two young songwriters who had been pitching their songs to London publishers without much success. They saw Tom and the band play in Caerphilly and thought them the ideal group to record demos. Ideal they weren't: expensive rehearsals were booked but the band didn't show up. Finally a tape was made, but London proved resistant to its charms until one Joe Meek took an interest. Meek, legendary maverick and madcap producer of 'Telstar' (a 1962 number one instrumental), recorded some tracks with the band, and a single, 'Lonely Joe' was planned, with a Godfrey/Glastonbury song as the B-side. But Meek delayed release and then stopped returning calls. The relationship ended in tempers and tears and the single never came out, Meek keeping the tapes. He famously committed suicide in 1967. Tommy and the Senators lost faith in Godfrey and Glastonbury, who agreed to relinquish their management rights in exchange for 5% of future earnings. It was just as well then that Mills and Tom arranged a meeting, through mutual friends. Many "mutual friends" have since claimed credit, but most plausible were Gordon Jones (who'd been at school with Mills) and local singer Johnny Bennett.

Mills was looking for an act that he could help to break big. Tom wanted to be that act. When they met, one Sunday lunchtime at a club in Porth, Mills thought Tom rather scruffy, though he realised he made more of an effort on stage. And that everybody he spoke to was urging him to discover this singer. Tom had already adopted an approach as flexible as his

---

LEFT: Tommy Scott and the Senators, rough diamonds dreaming of glory.

hips, usually wearing his black leather for younger crowds and suits or tuxes for more conservative ones. That evening Mills and his wife went along to the Senators' jam-packed show at Cwmtellery's Top Hat. It was so busy that the big-shot from London had to stand by the bar near the back. But he soon knew it was worth the crush. He's said that he knew within the first few bars that Tom's voice was going to be one of the greatest on earth. Maybe he was helped along to this epiphany by the band's shrewd, flattering decision to open with that aforementioned Gordon Mills song, 'I'll Never Get Over You'. They then launched into a scorching rendition of Ben E. King's 'Spanish Harlem'. Mills began planning how to get Tom to London as soon as possible.

Tom wasn't reluctant. Mills came to an agreement with Godfrey and Glastonbury (although later legal wranglings reared up) and guaranteed him a hit. He rolled up his sleeves and took charge. Tom trusted his experience, insights and instincts.

London, however, narrowed its eyes and demanded more convincing. As there was another Tommy Scott active in the big city, Mills re-christened our man Tom Jones. This emphasised his Welshness – a unique selling point, of sorts, at the time – and cashed in on the racy 1963 Tony Richardson-directed hit film of the same name. Mills also ditched the name The Senators, rebranding them The Playboys. He clearly had an eye and ear for Swinging Sixties London. So Tom Jones (leaving his wife and son for the first time) and The Playboys arrived in London, throbbing with dreams. It wasn't to be a case of overnight bright-lights-big-city glamour though. They were all placed in a not-exactly-luxurious two-room flat in Ladbroke Grove, with scarcely a penny between them. Yet they could see the ladder to the stars now. They just needed to figure out how it was to be climbed. Given a pound a day each to survive on, they dealt with the basics first. Such as, crucially: should they spend that pound on food, or booze?

Tom and the band's first single, 'Chills And Fever', came out in August 1964. And while it's now recognized as a visceral gem, it completely flopped upon release. Even before that landmark, the boys found that London just kept on dishing out trials, tribulations and disappointments. Gordon Mills' overdraft grew as he spent the three grand he'd made in royalties for writing the Johnny Kidd and The Pirates hit, and his wife's earnings as a model fell after daughter Tracey was born. Tom Jones and The Playboys landed a prime early gig supporting The Rolling Stones at Oxford Street's famous 100 Club, but it didn't instantly lead to anything. Gigs paid around £40, which wasn't chicken-feed then, but there weren't enough of them to suffice. (Tom's wife Linda got a job in the old glove factory back in Wales, to feed herself and their son). Recording the odd demo passed the time in the big city, but mostly the Valley boys were broke and stuck for something to do.

When they could afford to go out, they'd head to nearby Hammersmith for a Saturday night knees-up. They had youth on their side, but only up to a point. Vernon Hopkins was now 24, as was Tom. Guitarist Mickey Gee was 21, as was rhythm guitarist Dave Cooper. At 17, school-leaver Chris Slade, the drummer, was the baby of the band. Gee had quit a job in a Cardiff brewery to join the fame-chase. Hopkins had left his position as a printer at the *Pontypridd Observer*. They all accepted they'd been better off, financially, back home, but a team spirit kept them going; as did the occasional arrival of hampers and parcels of sandwiches from family and friends. Gee once confessed, "It wasn't very hip to be Welsh in those days." Six months went by. At least Tom was the only one with a wife and child hoping for support. He felt depressed at his inability to do so. He's said that on one bad day in Notting Hill he considered throwing himself under a tube train. Another time Vernon Hopkins found him crying and talking about suicide in the flat. Hopkins delivered a pep talk, but Tom muttered of giving up his dreams and going back to Wales. When he asked Mills (whose wife was pregnant again) if he could lend him five pounds to send to Linda, and realised that even Gordon – having stretched himself to keep the group in town – didn't have it, things looked on the grim side. Tom's admitted this was the worst period of his life.

"Linda's always been wonderful when times were rough," he later said. "She always believed in me as a singer and gave me encouragement to go on trying. She knew that singing was what I wanted to do in life. If you want to get somewhere in this business, you have to gamble."

Nevertheless, even at 24, in a competitive game, Tom, hair slicked back, wasn't perceived as by any means young for a potential pop star. Certain showbiz habits he'd picked up in homeland clubs were deemed old-fashioned, "too adult" or "too Fifties rock'n'roll". The newer pop stars were cute-faced, fey, boy-like. Tom was very blatantly a swarthy, bulky, man. To further frustrate matters, another band called The Playboys made a mark about town, and the Welshmen now had to find yet another name. They became The Squires.

So a lot rode on the debut single. Released by Decca, 'Chills And Fever', a Thompson/Gray composition, was and still is an exciting, all-action upbeat number with an incredibly powerful vocal by Tom. Somehow, critics and radio stations didn't warm to it. "Over-produced", claimed one. So sadly, despite excellent sales in Pontypridd, it stalled. "I honestly thought I'd had my big chance and failed," Tom remarked in an interview, years on, with the benefit of perspective. "I was pretty miserable then. You work hard for a recording break, and then when you get it you think you're on your way. But it's only the beginning of the battles."

A big break was just around the corner.

OPPOSITE: Tom, re-christened Tom Jones by Gordon Mills.

2
TOM JONES FEVER

Lady Luck was about to smile. Tom, having survived the drought, was about to be showered in success. Mills, just as the boys were starting to doubt his Svengali powers, came good. Yet it took a twist of fate, and a strange decision by Sandie Shaw, to make it so.

Mills had penned a song with another talented writer, Les Reed. (Reed was later to be involved with such Tom landmarks as 'Delilah', 'I'm Coming Home' and 'Daughter Of Darkness'). However, it had come about as they'd been commissioned to write the fast-rising Sandie Shaw a follow-up hit to her chart-topping 'Always Something There To Remind Me'. It was the kind of high-profile commission any songwriter would leap at, and Gordon had. To make a demo of the song, he'd hired The Squires, booking them into a Denmark Street studio. They knocked it out in 20 minutes.

It wasn't quite working: its odd, bossa nova-like rhythms weren't perfect yet. Still, every member of the band loved the song and believed they could make a hit of it. To appease them, Mills said that if Sandie Shaw turned it down, they could have it. He didn't for a second really think she'd do that. She did. And suddenly Tom and the band were set to record the irresistible 'It's Not Unusual' as a single.

Only it wasn't as simple as that. Mills needed a hit as badly as they did, and in his opinion the band were struggling to best present the song. He retained complete faith in Tom's voice, but had doubts about the musicians. From this point, they were to be used as Tom's backing band. The act was Tom. For a new session at Decca studios in West Hampstead, he and the label brought in session men, and The Ivy League as backing singers. After takes aplenty, it still didn't sound right until the now-iconic brass parts were hurled in by Peter Sullivan. Some present, including Tom, wondered if this was a smart move given the current ascendancy of electric guitars, but fears about what might be fashionable were over-ridden as, let's face it, it sounded great.

The rest of 1964 played out in a state of hope and nervousness as Decca delayed the release of 'It's Not Unusual' until January. Mills had no money to keep the band in London any longer – not even their daily pound – and told them to return to Wales for Christmas. He and his wife then tragically lost their unborn second baby. Privately, he wondered if his fellow Welshmen, who doubted Decca would fully get behind their single, would bother to come back. Yet Tom was optimistic as he reunited with his family in his mother-in-law's Cliff Terrace basement. 1965 was going to be a good year to be alive.

In late January 1965 'It's Not Unusual' finally emerged, but, in a slight that now sounds like high praise, was deemed "too hot" by BBC Radio. Its heat was fine by the more progressive types at Radio Caroline and Radio Luxembourg. The latter's Alan Freeman, who later declared it "a pop landmark" – put it straight onto the playlist. The way the man – compared at the time to P.J. Proby – sang, "Why can't this crazy love be mine?" could

LEFT: With his first hit arriving, Tom's career was in rude health.

OPPOSITE: Going up. Tom takes the first steps to superstardom.

not be ignored. Tom appeared on TV shows, including huge promotional opportunities like *Ready, Steady, Go!* and *Top Gear*, and the single swept into the charts at number 21. By early February it was at number 15. (The singles charts moved a lot more slowly back in those days). He gained a lot more live bookings, and soon became the first Welsh singer since Maureen Evans to grace the top ten. On 1 March – coincidentally St David's (the patron saint of Wales) Day – 'It's Not Unusual' took the step from number two to number one. Celebrations ensued. Mr Jones – on tour that night – may have had a drink or two. He may even have drunk till dawn.

He was still thought better-behaved than American UK exile Proby, whose trousers were known for splitting onstage. When Proby lost his slot on Liverpool singing star Cilla Black's UK tour, Tom was offered it. Gordon Mills coached him on how much wanton groin-thrusting was allowed, and when and where to rein it in. He enjoyed the tour with the ever-popular Cilla, and Tommy Roe of 'Dizzy' fame, and won over disgruntled Proby fans along the way. He was mobbed more than once by over-keen girls, and in one venue had to wriggle out of his coat and leave the young ladies clutching onto it as he ran for safety. (His most embarrassing moment came when he went to the toilet at an M1 services station, and some overheated girls "jumped over the door"). The Squires rode along for the adventure, even though they weren't on the record. Their days of surviving on a pound were, they thought, behind them now.

Overnight fame wasn't all wine and roses. Mills' first press release for Tom had read, "He's 22, he's a single, and he's a miner!" All patently untrue, even if it was what the screaming girls wanted to hear. When you hit number one during the week of your eighth wedding anniversary, the papers can be quick to 'expose' the facts. Tiger Tom was married with a son – what a scandal! The singer was embarrassed though, more because he felt it was unfair on Linda and Mark than anything else. Linda herself felt a shy misfit with regard to the showbiz world, but understood that 'sex sells' and libido was a part of the marketing of her husband. She witnessed the way his father was congratulated by his work-mates at the mines, and smiled as they showed him newspapers with Tom's picture and downed champagne and whisky, repeating, "Look, your Tom's got a number one!" Tom Junior felt like the cat who'd got the cream. The shrewd Gordon Mills was already working out how best to ensure his discovery was not a one-hit wonder.

RIGHT: The way the man sang "Why can't this crazy love be mine?" could not be ignored. 'It's Not Unusual' hit number one on 1 March, coincidentally St David's Day.

" *'He's 22, he's single and he's a miner!' read Gordon Mills'*
first press release for Tom. All patently untrue,
even if it was what the screaming girls wanted to hear… "

As the world now knows, Tom Jones was anything but a one-hit wonder. He cracked it.

Importantly, he quickly 'conquered' America, Mills working with supreme effectiveness. He lined up appearances for Tom on the influential Stateside favourite *The Ed Sullivan Show*, which had previously launched the Beatles to US audiences. With 'It's Not Unusual' released there in April '65, hopes were high. There was at first some resistance though. Ed Sullivan's producers still leaned towards the cautious, and elements in the mid-West deemed rock'n'roll the devil's music. Elvis and his pelvis still shocked some, so the Welshman was warned that cameramen would only shoot him from the waist up unless he kept the groin-thrusts under control. Tiger Tom wisely played the role of mildly frisky tomcat.

Yet as American radio locked on to 'It's Not Unusual' (it climbed into the Top Ten), his super-soulful voice had many convinced he was a black singer. Many black stations enthusiastically agreed to interview him: even when Mills and his team came clean, they assumed they were kidding. They had a surprise in store. And a surprise greeted Tom when he met up with soul legend Dionne Warwick, whom he'd recently met briefly in London, on his first visit to New York. As a soul fan he asked her to take him to the Harlem Apollo, the East Coast home of rhythm and blues music. Once there, he looked around and realised he was the only white man in the building. But he loved it there, and American soul singers have always loved him. It's all about the unrestrained, candid, sexually charged voice. Tom Jones is not English. He went down well on a marathon coast-to-coast tour organised by Dick Clark, the fabled DJ.

He'd already come a long way in a short time from Pontypridd to New York, and Mills and his wife requested/ordered that Tom and Linda join them on holiday in the South of France to relax and take in everything that had happened since the fateful release of 'It's Not Unusual'. On visits to Wales, his mother urged respect and caution, taking him aside and telling him, "Listen, Tommy boy – you might be a big shot up in London, but here in Pontypridd you wipe your shoes when you come in, you're good to your wife, and you take your turn bringing in the coal." Yet after years of being penniless, Tom exercised the inalienable right of the nouveaux riches to spend big and to spend ostentatiously as the dividends of success accumulated.

PREVIOUS PAGES: Tom poses with his wife at home in 1967.
Tom sits with his publicist Chris Hutchins, while travelling to a concert in Blackpool.

LEFT: Sixties icons (left to right) Paul McCartney, Dusty Springfield, Tom Jones and Ringo Starr.

To live the dream. First he bought a much-coveted S-type Jaguar. Then, a home near the river Thames in Shepperton, Middlesex, near London. For Tom, Linda and young Mark it made a dramatic contrast to life in Linda's parents' basement. The house cost eight thousand pounds, and was described as "bright, dashing, modern, with plenty of room and lots of fresh air". It was also described by some papers as "a mansion". It was about the size of the entire terrace he'd been raised in. This was the Sixties: it revelled in a cream-carpeted lounge and a long sofa decked out in orange and black Thai silk. Grand, yes, but within a year it proved insufficient for these fast risers, so they moved a few miles away to Sunbury-on-Thames and an even grander twenty-five thousand pound abode.

Tom Jones has always lived the pop star role to the full: there was to be no false modesty or self-effacing shrinking violet act from him when it came to image or luxurious trappings. As for the Squires, they resided together not in a mansion but in a semi-detached house in Hounslow. No Jag for them: they shared a van. They were very much the 'backing band' now, and within their ranks the first flickers of resentment wrestled with their elementary enjoyment of touring and appearing on TV.

Meanwhile Mills, ever-vigilant and shrewd, was nurturing the publicity side of things and had much of his focus on those potentially huge American audiences.

PREVIOUS PAGES: Tom's swinging; Tom's smokin'.

OPPOSITE: 'What's New Pussycat?' – Tom takes a leopard for a walk.

ABOVE: Digging for victory in his show This is Tom Jones.

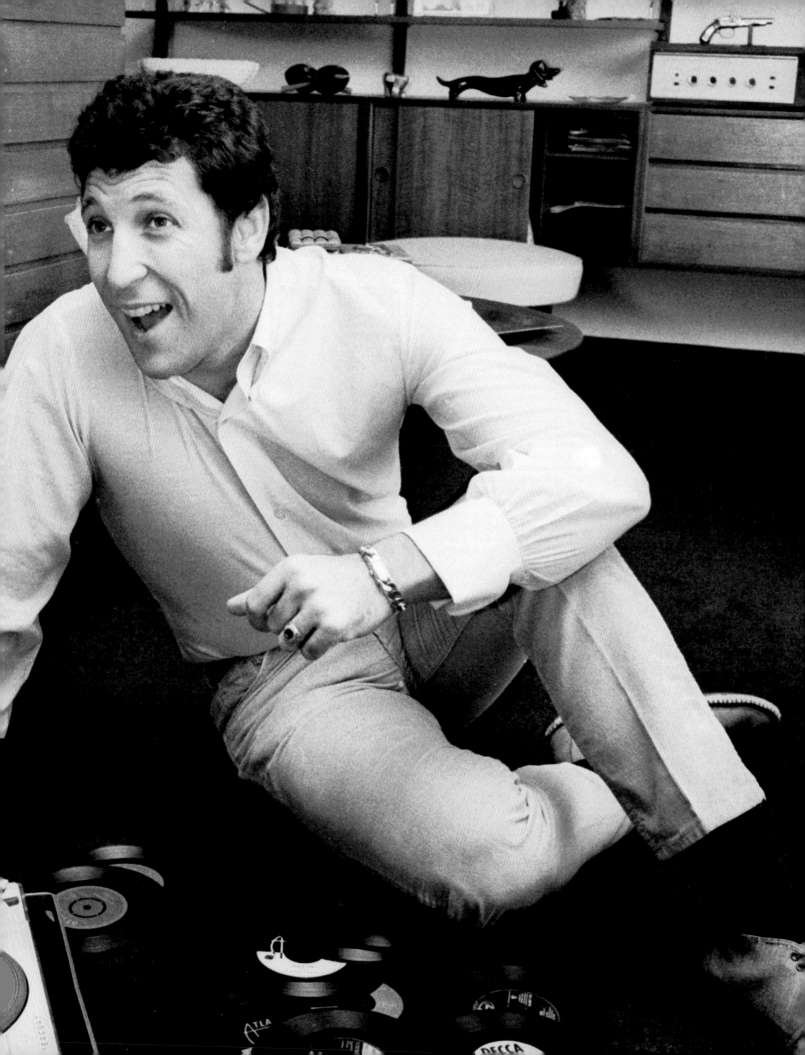

Nowadays rather overlooked, two more minor hit singles next came along in the shape of 'Once Upon A Time' and (avowed Elvis Presley favourite) 'With These Hands', but Mills had his ears pricked for a song to make more of a splash.

Tiger Tom was about to get in touch with the world's inner feline again. 'What's New Pussycat?' was the theme song to a swinging Sixties sex farce, a film written by (and co-starring) an up-and-coming Woody Allen. It was riddled with innuendo and sauce. Who could be more perfect to belt it out than Mr Jones? As Peter Sellers, Peter O'Toole and Ursula Andress battled with a

spluttering script, everyone remembered the song more than they remembered the movie. Little wonder, as it was penned by the master song-writing pair Burt Bacharach and Hal David. At this point they'd already blessed the decade with classics such as 'Walk On By' (for Tom's new friend Dionne), 'Make It Easy On Yourself', 'Anyone Who Had A Heart' (for Tom's old friend Cilla) and 'Baby It's You'. 'What's New Pussycat?' was their first successful film score, and the title song gained an Oscar nomination for Best Song, only to be beaten at the line by 'The Shadow Of Your Smile" (from the film *The Sandpiper*). The sleevenotes to a later re-release of the

---

PREVIOUS PAGES: *Dressing the part; spinning the latest 45s.*   OPPOSITE: *Tom was staring into the lens of fame .*   ABOVE: *The Squires feared being left behind in the giddy rush.*

soundtrack album capture the buzz of that moment: "The choice of new Welsh heartthrob Tom Jones for the title track was… inspired. Earlier in the year he had a hit with the brassy 'It's Not Unusual', and a titillating post-Elvis lounge-rock sex symbol was born. He was the perfect voice and image for the romping song." It raced to number three, Stateside.

Pauline Kael, the renowned film critic, once summed up the movies as "kiss kiss, bang bang". Tom's career seemed to have that as a motif now. Another spectacular 1965 film title song came his way in the shape of

'Thunderball', from the fourth James Bond 007 adventure. This was the Connery-as-Bond era, and the song, written by John Barry and Don Black, was suitably stylish and suave (if overtly straining to echo 'Goldfinger'.) The lyrics, about a macho yet magnetic villain, are crooned with supreme relish by Jones. You can hear him relating. "They call him the winner who takes all….he will break any heart without regret…" The song stands up well today, a proud, portentous, pulsating big ballad. And another huge hit for Tom.

There are risks for rockers who step into big-ballad territory, however raunchy and sinister those ballads. Some critics were already getting sniffy about his credibility, pulling out accusations of "selling out". To be fair to them, this was the heyday of social 'revolution' against old-fashioned social mores, or at least of mild,

PREVIOUS PAGES: Learning to drive; Captain Fantastic; Tom and Dusty Springfield meet the Queen.

BELOW: Tom and son jump for joy. RIGHT: Tom tries the 'smart casual' look.

middle-class rebellion. Working-class Jones was well aware of the barbs calling him "square". "True," he allowed. "What I'd really like is to release a big bluesy R&B number, just to show everyone I can still do it. But my manager points out the snags to me, and I think maybe he's right and I should stick to what I've been doing." It was a theme, a nagging desire, which Tom was to revisit later in his long career. For now, he added, "I realise I'm becoming known as a film-song performer…I'm considering going into movies myself." The latter thought never really blossomed into reality, partly because this "sell-out" was soon a tax exile, and partly because early '66 saw him forcibly rested to recover from having his tonsils removed. (He was relieved to find his voice was unaffected). One can't help wishing some sharp director had cast him then, in the mid-Sixties, in a role suitable to his charismatic, cocky persona. Instead of hollering at Hollywood, he went to win at Vegas.

In 1966 Gordon Mills was perturbed that, despite Tom Jones' international fame growing relentlessly, and the honour of a Grammy award for Best New Artist, he hadn't lit up the British singles charts for a while. Yet it was Tom who found the song to rectify that glitch. It wasn't one to shoo away the notion that he was turning 'square', but it was to prove one of his most enduringly emotive recordings.

Tom had always admired Jerry Lee Lewis, and hearing 'The Green, Green Grass Of Home' on Lewis' album *Country Songs For City Folks*, he felt a chord being struck. The song is still, now, an unofficial national anthem in Wales. Tom's beautifully interpreted version, released as a single, rose to number one (Tom's second) in the UK and stayed there for so long that its sticking power became a newspaper-and-television talking point. It also sold in vast numbers in America, winning over the country music heartland of Nashville. Jerry Lee, when Tom played him his rendition, grinned happily and guaranteed his biggest fan it'd be a million-seller. 'The Killer''s only error, it turned out, was under-estimating its appeal.

A less satisfying side effect was that it opened up a country-and-western market for Tom that he was to pursue in subsequent periods. And those who disliked the 'square' and his weepy ballads had more ammunition. *Melody Maker* observed that it was "the song the hippies love to hate", then, warming to its theme, declared that "the sob story of 'that old oak tree that I used to play on'" brought forth "a barrage of spleen from the self-appointed arbiters of teenage taste".

RIGHT: Hits like 'Thunderball' kept on coming.

OPPOSITE: 'The Green, Green Grass Of Home' landed Tom his second UK number one.

Tom wasn't unduly bothered by any snipes. As he'd chosen the song himself, he smiled, "At least it's proved I can pick my own winners." He went on, perhaps baiting the radicals, "It's shown that I can slow down a bit. I don't necessarily have to belt them out. I don't cater for the teenage screamers any more. I do polished shows." The quote reveals much. He was consciously, deliberately, moving in the direction of career longevity: no fleetingly hot one-hit wonders here. As he accepted a gold disc for 'The Green, Green Grass Of Home' live on stage on TV during *Sunday Night At The London Palladium*, he must have felt completely vindicated. It was the

year's only million-seller in the UK, and with 1966 also seeing England win the World Cup for the only time, something of a nationally-iconic pop landmark. In Wales, it resonated even more stirringly, with its presumably unintentional echoes of the Richard Llewelyn novel *How Green Was My Valley* (a story centred around life in a tiny mining village) underscoring the sentiments. Wales, the land of song, had, and adored, its biggest ever star.

ere would always be a welcome for him there, however much he took to America, and it to him.

Later the same year, those critics saying Tom couldn't rock any more received a disarming, driven riposte. He released the Mills-penned hit 'Not Responsible', a short, sharp shock of electric energy and lippy lust, every bit as fired up as 'Chills And Fever'.

In October 1966 Tom Jones had consolidated his American buzz by announcing a month of high-profile Las Vegas shows, proudly announcing that he followed "Tony Bennett and Andy Williams into this new club…" The new club was no less than Caesar's Palace. Of The

LEFT: Tom visits Berchtesgaden, Germany at a reception to celebrate the sale of a million Tom Jones records.

BELOW LEFT: Taking a well-earned tea break.

BELOW RIGHT: Leaving very little to the imagination.

Squires, only young drummer Chris Slade (who'd been improving in leaps and bounds after drum lessons in London) was to be taken along to play with the American band line-up. These shows never came to be, however. A new time – Spring 1967 – and venue – The Flamingo – was to replace them. And these proved to be life-changing, career-defining concerts. The rest of the Sixties were to be primarily Tom's 'Vegas period'. Square, maybe, but glitzy and hugely remunerative. He took up home in the American album charts and his energetic, glamorous gigs hot-footed it into showbiz folklore.

He'd perfected his act with well-received shows at London's Talk Of The Town. Now reports ran that he was to collect a cool (and then-almost-incredible) million dollars for three months of shows in Vegas and New York. He told the *NME*, "It feels really, really great, but the offer means more to me than the money itself. It shows they have real faith in me as an artist."

Gordon Mills had useful contacts in America, though perhaps it was his wife Jo who came up with some vital advice now. As a former Bluebell Girl in Vegas, she knew how the city's fame snakes-and-ladders worked. She warned Gordon not to accept the offers from smaller venues, hotels, and bars that were raining in, as once you settled for a lower rung it was hard to climb to higher levels. The Mills wanted Tom to hit the highest peaks of stardom, headlining huge clubs. When Tom went down a storm (especially with the ladies) at the Copacabana in New York and the Deauville in Miami, they knew he (and they) could pull it off. And so a top-billing residency at Vegas' The Flamingo was booked. The Flamingo was a sleeping giant of sorts, once legendary but recently ailing. New management, led by the memorably-monikered Nick Naff, were bent on hyping it to the heavens. Which was, naturally, fine by Gordon. The residency was to last for an astounding, triumphant, 18 months, after which point the show had to be relocated to bigger and bigger venues.

Initial promotion was a master-class. The phrase "Tom Jones Fever" was coined by Naff, leading to a similarly-named album (*The Tom Jones Fever Zone*). He positioned bottles of "Tom Jones fever pills" on the club's tables, pitching that they might not cure you but they'd possibly keep your fever under some degree of control. A strategically-positioned ambulance sat flashily at the back of the venue, just in case the fever got too much for the more faint-hearted. Commercials on the radio during the lead-in kept the public up to date on what temperature

PREVIOUS PAGES: "The old home town looks the same…"

LEFT: Tom meets hero Elvis Presley and his young wife Priscilla at the Flamingo Hotel, Las Vegas, 1968.

Tom Jones Fever had reached that day. This was hype as an art form.

And remember how Mills had taken the name Tom Jones from the tastefully bawdy film? Conveniently, coincidentally, a musical stage show adaptation now opened just along the Strip in Vegas. Some may have been confused, but more were just encouraged by the local ubiquity of the name and its connotations of sensual indulgence. Tom could walk through the lobby of The Flamingo untroubled only for the first few nights. From then on, he didn't dare to unless he wanted to be chased by hysterical wild-eyed fans, his body grabbed at and his hair pulled.

Alan Walsh, a British journalist, wrote an article headlined "Tom, Toast Of Vegas", in which he noted that Duke Ellington had gone out of his way to attend the

opening night, and that a special show was swiftly arranged to satisfy the curiosity of celebrities who were in town. "It seems that one of the stars in the audience will be Frank Sinatra, who is taking an interest in Tom's career." So was one Elvis Presley…

Tom Jones was now not so much a star, more a phenomenon, a sensation. Forget "square": Mills had cottoned on early that adults had more money to splash out on entertainment than did teenagers. America had bought in. The States feted him, and he fell in love in return.

If Tom Jones was the new prince, Elvis Presley remained the king. Gordon Mills had warmed up the press nicely by suggesting in '67 that he was "in talks" with Colonel Tom Parker, Elvis' controversial manager and a man whose approach and work ethic Mills admired. Mills spread word that The Colonel had been watching

---

PREVIOUS PAGES: Sharing a laugh with Sandie Shaw; Tom on Broadway.

OPPOSITE: Skateboarding in London.

ABOVE: Just one of the awards Tom would win during his long career.

NEXT PAGE: Tom belts out a tune to a rapt audience.

Tom's progress, and was keen to get involved in his US management. In truth, he was just available for advice and consultation, but Mills smartly played up the connection. It was a link that really took off when Elvis started coming to Tom's shows in Vegas.

Tom had briefly met Presley in 1965 on his first visit to the States, and had been somewhat in awe of his idol, and uncharacteristically shy. Now, Elvis was specifically coming to see him, in action, and his already high confidence welcomed another boost. Elvis didn't simply show up once to appease management; he kept on coming back. When he made his own historic Vegas comeback (in black leather), Nick Naff wasn't afraid to say he'd copped several of Tom's moves and incorporated them into his act.

After the exuberant 18 months at the Flamingo, Tom's show moved on (and upwards) to a venue thrice the size, The International; where Elvis himself had now made that legendary comeback. Even this wasn't a big enough room, and Tom soon moved on again to Caesar's Palace. He was also slotting in huge shows in New York, breaking Frank Sinatra's record, which had stood since the Fifties, for box office takings at the Copacabana. One review from here raved, "Women screamed, stomped, went limp. Girls seemed to shudder with rapture. There was swinging Tom, doing the sorts of things, pelvically speaking, that few fans will ever see…" And Tom was achieving all this while still enjoying the party lifestyle, knocking back champagne after shows in Vegas, carousing till dawn, then sleeping most of the day until hurling himself into another full-throttled performance.

BELOW: U.S. television fell in love with Tom.

OPPOSITE: Tom arrives in Paris for a concert at the Olympia music hall.

As the Sixties spun to a climax, Tom Jones' international celebrity stature had reached a peak which is hard to overstate. Don't forget he also had his own successful TV shows: *The Tom Jones Show* was a prime-time British hit from February 1969, and screened Stateside too. It was axed in January 1971, to the shock of many, before its second season had concluded, having dropped out of the US top 20 after a ratings battle with the Raymond Burr detective show, *Ironside*. But when it was big, it was very big. Guests were stellar, and included hero-turned-friend Jerry Lee Lewis, Burt Bacharach, Johnny Cash, Perry Como, Janis Joplin, Cleo Laine, the Bee Gees and the Moody Blues. Even the era's leading female sex symbol, movie star Raquel Welch, joined the era's leading male sex symbol for a lively rock'n'roll duet. (When Tom brags on *The Voice* of having duetted

with some all-time greats, he's not kidding). Such link-ups only added more glamour to his reputation. In fact, it was more a case of the other stars needing to be associated with his glory. When half a dozen shows were shot in Los Angeles by ABC, thirty thousand ticket applications flooded the studio.

Well-known and influential impresario Lew Grade was backing the shows, paying Jones an incredible nine million pounds and at first promising 80 of them. "The greatest singer in the world", he announced. To this day many are baffled as to why the show wasn't allowed to run and run.

Tom and Gordon weren't overly concerned, as their bank accounts brimmed with healthy glows. Another house-move was on the cards for the Jones family, with Tom moving Linda and Mark from Sunbury to a vast mansion in Weybridge. He gave his old Shepperton home (and a car) to his parents. His father learned to drive at age 56, to facilitate visits to his homeland. Now and again, he'd borrow one of his son's Mercedes or Rolls Royces.

OPPOSITE: Psyching himself up for those Caesar's Palace shows.

BELOW: A close shave.

The hits had kept on coming too. In 1967 both 'Detroit City' and 'I'm Coming Home' climbed the UK charts. The former bore a country twang. The latter, a gorgeous romantic ballad lovingly sung, was co-written by Les Reed, who'd written 'It's Not Unusual' with Mills. And Reed again came good as co-writer of '68's massive hit, 'Delilah', which reached number two. Despite being a rather eerie, melodramatic tale of murder and a crime of passion, it's another Jones hit which has since taken on a life of its own, its baroque chorus routinely hollered out at big sporting occasions. 1968's other jewel was '(It Looks Like) I'll Never Fall In Love Again', with Tom playing the broken-hearted victim but doing so with another breathtaking vocal that even today sounds like it might melt your ears. The albums were constantly ticking over nicely: 'Delilah' gave its title to a September 1968 number one and one of his biggest sellers. He had never quite mastered the albums market, releasing too many piece-meal compilations and live offerings, but they all did respectably, and between 1966 and 1971 he was rarely absent from the charts. In America, where his tireless touring was always boosting sales, things were even better. There were times during 1969 where he had five or more albums in the charts simultaneously. Make no mistake, Tom Jones' Sixties were finishing on an almighty high, and he strode into the Seventies like a swaggering colossus.

LEFT: Tens of thousands applied for tickets when Tom recorded his TV specials.

" Make no mistake, Tom finishing on an almighty into the Seventies like a

Jones' 1960s were high, and he strode swaggering colossus."

3

INTO THE
SWINGING SEVENTIES

Tom's career had caught fire. The Sixties weren't ending quite so happily for The Squires, his former close buddies and hometown backing band, who'd originally chased the grail to London with him, sharing squalid accommodation as well as sandwiches and pints. "Tom Jones Fever" had given them some chills. Four years as the little-noted, scarcely-used backing band may not have been their dream, but they'd gone along with it, smart enough to acknowledge that the shows and parties they were seeing were more exciting than life back in the valleys had been. Vernon Hopkins, for instance, met Elvis and Priscilla Presley at one Vegas show. Yet it was obvious that the clock was ticking against them, and that Tom's fame was now edging them towards the exit door.

When it came, The Squire's departure was tied in to the reappearance of former managers Godfrey and Glastonbury, who couldn't fail to have noticed Tom's global ascent and his seven-figure earnings. They wanted their piece of the financial pie. Five per cent was their agreed due, but they sued, stating that Gordon Mills hadn't handed over a halfpenny. Legal wrangles being inevitably complex, the case had taken five years to get to court. In January 1969 the London High Court heard arguments until an out-of-court settlement was reached.

Mills was disgruntled, and saw The Squires as, along with the ex-managers, part of the old regime, and baggage to be shaken off. Hopkins has said the atmosphere around court was frosty, and he felt Tom wasn't his usual self with him in the pub (where else?) afterwards. Mills took Hopkins aside and, using his charm skills, said he had a song for The Squires to record while Tom took a well-earned holiday. Hopkins probed, and learned that Tom was to focus on American and television activities, meaning there was little need for The Squires. They were to be let go. Their subsequent single, given no promotion and a cold press-and-radio response, sank without trace. Hopkins didn't see Jones for another five years.

Melody Maker ran the PR soft-soap piece they were given by Mills. "A spokesman told us The Squires have been with Tom Jones right from the start but there are two reasons why they have now amicably parted. Firstly, Tom will be spending much of the year making his television series, and any tours he does are now with the Ted Heath Orchestra – so the group wouldn't be working with him for a long time. Secondly, for some time now the group has had ambitions to try and make it on their own. They are making a bid for the Top Thirty themselves, with a record produced by Tom's manager Gordon Mills. It is a cover version of Joe South's American hit 'Games People Play', rush-released tomorrow."

So much for the musketeer spirit; the Welsh bonds were broken. Games people play, indeed. Of course the split made solid sense on every level, but as a new decade began Jones had to pull off some nifty footwork to prove he wasn't losing touch with his roots.

In January 1969 a perceptive if teasing article in the *Observer* stated that Tom had sold 26 million records already, and that his television show was costing three thousand pounds per minute. It suggested that as a vocalist he was "A rabble-rouser. In days when nice little pop stars are still mods, he is unashamedly a rocker. He is the mum's Mick Jagger, the performing bear of the middle-class audience. For those who can't or don't want to understand the more subtle happenings of pop, the no-nonsense corn of Jones the miner's son has an immediate and obvious appeal."

There was truth in this: 'The Green, Green Grass Of Home' had held the number one spot despite competition from hits by more critically-revered acts like the Small Faces, The Kinks, The Beach Boys and Manfred Mann. The article also contained the interesting information that, in his mansion, Tom had a collection of 12 guns, over 50 knives and some swords. Calling him "green-eyed Tiger Tom", it went on "(he) appeals to the mature woman.

With his George Raft sideburns and Sicilian Sunday suit, this self-confessed ex-drunkard, ex-Teddy Boy and ex-mini gangster, who used to wear a ring in the shape of a skull and crossbones, roars around the stage like some bubbling Quatermass monster, seizing every song by the scruff of the neck, rattling it about and, eventually, choking it to death."

The more sarcastic comments were perhaps motivated by the feeling that Jones was out of fashion in the more 'alternative' quarters of the rock world, with which he held little truck. In fact Tom poured fuel on the fire by saying of the era's hippies, "When I see them squatting with their banners in their sandals, I feel like telling them to get off their backsides and do something. They do nothing. They're bums." No Woodstock icon, our Tom.

He was certainly raking it in. He, Gordon Mills and Mills' latest successful singing star Engelbert Humperdinck had now all moved to houses within a mile of Weybridge. Previous/current residents of the

area included Paul McCartney, John Lennon and Cliff Richard. Gordon named his mansion Little Rhondda; Tom's was Torpoint, and boasted a swimming pool, gym complex and security staff. The Inland Revenue were, unsurprisingly, sniffing at the trio's accounts, so business mastermind Mills recommended they set up a record company, MAM. Mills' Midas touch ensured success. The first single release was Dave Edmunds' 'I Hear You Knocking', and it went to number one. Later Mills launched another chart-topping star, one Gilbert O'Sullivan (of 'Nothing Rhymed', 'Get Down', 'Clair' and 'Alone Again, Naturally' fame), who spent some of his earnings by buying a Mercedes from Mr Jones. 'Clair' was inspired by Gordon and Jo Mills' daughter.

Still the gang had to be canny with money. Labour came into power in 1974, and high-earners like Jones faced taxes swallowing up 80-90% of their income. So he spent increasing amounts of time in America, "for tax reasons". He and Mills owned a £750,000 private jet, and the MAM trio also bought a farm in Sussex. Tom though couldn't even visit it, as he now had to limit his trips back to Britain. This obviously affected family matters too: to see wife Linda and son Mark, Tom had to arrange meetings with them in territories like France or Belgium. He'd sometimes take the now adult Mark on tour with him, an experience that clearly served the boy well for later life.

It was just a matter of time before the once-broke, now-loaded boy from the valleys had to emigrate to America.

Tom didn't just move to the States; he did so in typically flamboyant, ostentatious style. He acquired his Green Card and persuaded Linda to join him in luxurious 'exile'. He bought an expensive estate, previously owned by none other than Rat Pack superstar Dean Martin, in LA's Bel Air. It cost him a cool million (dollars), and seven years later was worth seven million. He told the *Observer* the building was "conceived in 1939 and finished in 1940…just like me." He then bought houses in Beverly Hills for his parents and his sister, and another for his son Mark, who'd now married an American girl, Donna.

The (red-brick, unusually for the location) Bel Air mansion had 16 rooms and the biggest swimming pool in the highly desirable area. Showing he hadn't completely forgotten his roots, Tom had gilded Welsh dragons decorating the entrance gates. He shipped over his furniture from Tor Point and hung the walls with his gold records. To get to the pool you traversed a room serving as cinema or theatre. The grounds were adorned with African palms, camellias, oleanders and bougainvillea. Yet the crowning glory was that red

RIGHT: The trappings of success. Tom relaxes in his Bel Air mansion.

telephone kiosk he'd had imported – along with plenty of HP sauce – from his hometown. When in 1983 Mark's wife had a baby boy, Alexander, Tom's grandson, additions to the grounds included toy trains and cars and an Italian fountain. Yes, Tiger Tom was a granddad. In '87 a grand-daughter, Emma, came along. Tom beamed proudly, "When I play with my grandson it reminds me of what life's all about."

Gordon Mills had also moved to America, but by now was estranged from wife Jo, who remained in Weybridge. Engelbert Humperdinck had also by now split from Mills as a business partner. As if to match Tom for flash, Mills, pre-empting Michael Jackson, owned a private zoo, but couldn't accommodate all the animals in his new home. Five gorillas and seven orang-utans were generously donated to the San Diego Zoo. Strange but true: the first baby gorilla born in California for 20 years was thus given the name Gordon.

Tom was honest about the reasons for his relocation. In 1983 during a visit to the UK he told the *Daily Express*, "I could never have done it by staying home.

Depending on how you look at it, you can blame or credit Harold Wilson (Labour Prime Minister) with my success abroad." He said he'd been on tour when Labour swept in in '74, and Mills had phoned him in a frenzy, yelling, "Don't come back! The Labour government will tax you out of existence!" Perhaps aware of how 'posh Tory' this sounded, Jones added, "The laugh was, coming from a family of coalminers, we always voted Labour, no question. But my old dad, who died two years ago, said that if voting Tory would get his boy home, he'd do it – and he did. Which my mam still can't quite believe…"

His loyal father's death from emphysema in 1981 (aged 72) had the papers reporting that Tom had stayed at home and cried for several days. Tom senior had been able to retire early thanks to Tom's largesse. The singer was always generous with family. It seems he also felt keen to protest to the press that he'd been

---

ABOVE: Comparing wallets with Engelbert Humperdinck.

OPPOSITE: Settling into Dean Martin's old home.

extremely reluctant to leave Britain. In '76 the *People* ran an interview headlined "Why I'm Quitting The Green, Green Grass Of Home". He argued "I've been forced into exile and I don't like it one little bit. (The taxmen) really are a shower. They're cutting their own throats and they don't seem to realise it. Let's say I make two million dollars this year: if I lived at home, the government would take about 98% of that. Now I don't mind paying taxes, but 98% is just ridiculous. There's no incentive for me to earn large amounts of bread if it's all going to be eaten by the taxman. I don't like the hand I've been forced to play, but what can I do about it? I love Britain, it's home, but…"

There were, of course, compensations to the high life. By 1983 the five thousandth hotel room key thrown to the tax exile on stage by an admiring female was picked up from the Caesar's Palace stage, then framed in a light-hearted ceremony and hung in the lobby. Tom denied he'd ever taken advantage of any of the keys, laughing, "I mean, you never know what you might find on the other side of the door." Pressed on his love life, he claimed, "My wife isn't the jealous type. She asks no questions, so I tell no lies. That's the way it is."

Jones was wise to exercise caution with regard to "what you might find on the other side of the door". He admitted he always felt safer in Britain than in America. He kept up an impressive fitness regime in his personal gym, maintaining his physique by lifting weights for an hour a day, and obviously had minders. He'd been uncomfortable with the live-in guards at the mansion, but installed police-linked panic buttons and erected a huge wall around the grounds. Yet, concerned about

kidnappers and the like in the States, he wasn't slow to add to his gun collection. At Elvis Presley's suggestion, he often carried a handgun, saying it was necessary to protect his grandchildren. As late as 1992, he told *People* magazine, "You have to be aware you're vulnerable – in the States, especially, you have to have high security." He added that Elvis once gave him a "pistol" as a gift. "He carried a gun everywhere. Even on stage he used to conceal it in the small of his back." Perhaps one contributory factor to his nervousness was that, back in 1969, he'd found that his name had been included on the terrifying 'hit-list' of murderer Charles Manson

and his gang, along with the names of Elizabeth Taylor and Frank Sinatra. "Apparently," he recounted, "the plan was that a girl from his gang would come to one of my concerts, somehow 'get close' to me afterwards, and then try to kill me while 'giving me one'. In the moment of ecstasy. It was real scary. Manson was an aspiring songwriter and was jealous of anyone successful: I suppose he thought if he killed us all he'd stand a better chance." He mused sadly, "But like with John Lennon, if anyone really wanted to do something, I couldn't stop them."

Having given hippies short shrift, Jones, despite being an enthusiastic drinker, was always firmly anti-drugs.

OPPOSITE: *An unostentatious visit home to Wales.*

BELOW: *Nautical but nice. Filming in Barbados.*

NEXT PAGES: *The suave Sixties smoothie; the impassioned soul man.*

Even when friend-idol Elvis indulged, he was stern. When President Nixon bizarrely appointed Presley an official narcotics agent, Tom quipped, "He should have arrested himself." He elaborated on the matter: "I love what I do and I wouldn't want anything to get in the way of it. So I've always avoided drugs. I was brought up on light ale, and I've always believed pop is better than pot! With the occasional drink, you can consume it and not show it. Whereas with drugs, perfectly normal people are reduced to blithering idiots within minutes. Seeing people take drugs upsets me." It was said he'd walk out of a party if there were drugs around. "I've been at showbiz parties in very respectable hotels where I've been the only one drinking and everyone else was on drugs. But I reckon you can't be a performer and do drugs."

A memory from youth seems to have influenced this judgment. "The bass player in one of my early bands tried pot for the first time then went to pieces on stage. He was simply incapable of playing. He was all over the place. Couldn't even change chords. That shocked me."

However, Tom Jones was not presented to the public as a saint. For one of the leading sex symbols of the time, a media-led payback was inevitable. Tom's 'scandalous' extra-marital love life was regularly 'exposed' by the press from the mid-Sixties onwards. Some flings he's admitted. Other 'kiss-and-tell' purveyors have been rather more coldly dismissed. Yet through it all, his marriage has survived, for over half a century now. Tom Jones and Linda grew up in the old school.

"When you're in the process of making love," Jones once said in a surprisingly frank interview, "the woman seems everything to you. Afterwards, she's one of two things: someone you want to keep with you, or someone you want to crawl away from. A wife must be in the former category."

All this much unseemly scandal and titillation, of course, kept alive the enduring legend of Jones the Lothario, ensuring regular publicity boosts. Not all in the best possible taste, perhaps, but that career has been a lesson in longevity. Which, in pop music, IS unusual.

Tom Jones was asked about music-business longevity in 1987, and replied with a customary name-dropping anecdote. "Regarding my voice and work, Frank Sinatra told me twenty years ago that I'd never last, my voice would go, if I didn't change the way I sang. But what other way is there?" Of course his voice has been reined in over the years, but the attitude stands tall. "I'll be around until the green, green grass is turned into a car park," he laughed.

He's always made use of his tales of meetings with A-list stars, in recent years getting in on the joke and

LEFT Bring on the dancing girls. "I love what I do," said Tom.

introducing a wink and nod of self-mockery. One friendship he's always been visibly proud of, and never reluctant to talk about, is his old bond with the late great Elvis Presley. There seems to have been an authentic closeness between the two men. Elvis of course was Tom's idol as a young aspiring singer back in South Wales, while Elvis saw Tom's electrifying Las Vegas shows and was enthused enough to launch his own incendiary, revitalised late-Sixties comeback.

Their first encounter was back in 1965, when Colonel Tom Parker, Presley's manager, agreed that the up-and-coming Welshman could briefly meet his star at Paramount Studios in LA. Elvis was filming one of his movies. Tom waited anxiously beside the set. Then Parker gave the green light and before Tom could say anything, Elvis moved towards him. "He walked towards me singing 'With These Hands'. I couldn't believe it! Not only that, he knew every track on my album," recounted Tom gleefully. "He asked me how, coming from Wales, I sang like that. There I was, ready to tell him how much he'd influenced me, and he began telling me how much he liked my records!"

As Tom's star later rose, Elvis's career was on pause. He knew he wanted to come back strong in Vegas, and quietly arranged to watch Tom's shows there, as incognito as possible. He was dazzled, and the pair got on well again. Elvis would even sing 'Delilah' in his dressing-room as a pre-show warm-up.

ABOVE: Dropping in for a manly pint back home.

OPPOSITE: Kimono over to my place. Note the Welsh dragon.

Over the subsequent period of friendship, Elvis would confide in Tom and Tom claims to have felt "closer to him than any other entertainer". The pair would sing gospel songs together, like 'Amazing Grace'. For a while he hoped Elvis might help him make the leap into movie roles. But in 1992 he said ruefully, "I've never made a movie because the parts I'm offered never have any meat in them. I'm always offered these Elvis-type roles and, believe me, Elvis hated them himself. The thing that would have appealed to me would have been a part like one of *The Wild Bunch*. So I'll just stick to singing. Anyway, I've only ever wanted to rock."

He said that, but earlier in his career his team tried hard to get suitable film projects running. In '68 he'd told reporters, "I want to do films. I want audiences to recognise me." As often in Hollywood, things got stuck in development or lost in translation, despite his acclaimed TV presence. In '71 he was saying, "I've been a bit frightened, and stayed away from films. I don't want

people saying: 'oh, he's not such a good actor.' There was talk of making *The Gospel Singer*, from the novel by controversial writer Harry Crews. Jones (and Gordon Mills) had bought the rights. United Artists said they'd signed Jones to a three-film deal. Charlene Tilton from *Dallas* was mooted to co-star. It never came to fruition. However Harry Crews did say that Jones had worked up a great Southern accent. Jones said he'd been coached by Elvis.

By '76 he was being offered roles in the British sexploitation hit *The Stud*, which starred Joan Collins: the part went to Oliver Tobias when Tom and advisers thought it too risky, too controversial. Yet when Joan's sister Jackie (author of *The Stud*) published another novel, *Lovers And Gamblers*, it was rumoured that its tales of a promiscuous rocker who liked threesomes and whose shy son travelled with him on tour was based on…you've guessed it.

The almosts and not-quites kept coming in the film world, with a role as an assassin in *Yockowald* falling

---

OPPOSITE: Tom 'wins' a spoof sparring match with Muhammad Ali.

BELOW LEFT: Tom in fighting form.

BELOW RIGHT: A police escort at Heathrow Airport.

NEXT PAGE: Let them eat cake: Raquel Welch was among those queuing up for a birthday kiss from Mr Jones…

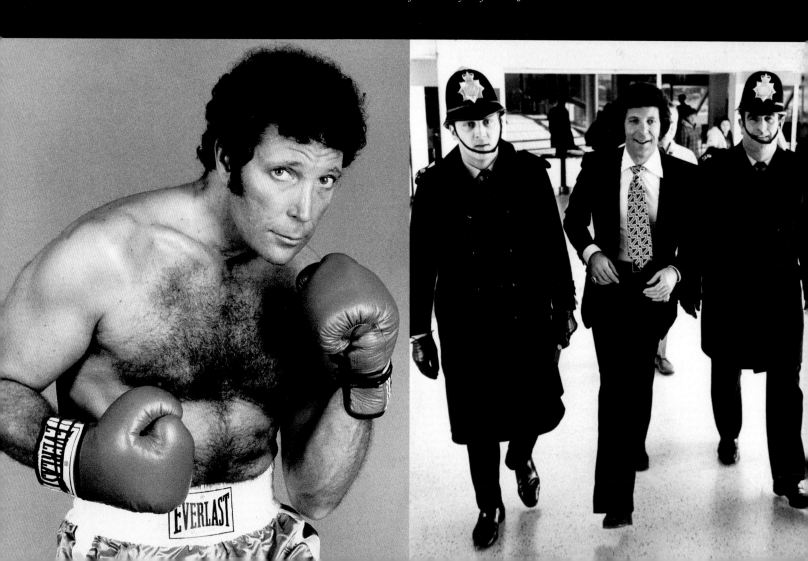

Happy Birthday

"I've never made a movie because the parts I get offered never have any meat in them…"

through after three weeks' shooting, due to financial problems. It's very demanding and different, said Tom of "this movie-making business." Aged 38 when *Yockowald* collapsed, he began to feel time wasn't on his side in this particular arena. He and Gordon gave a big push, starting a film production company as they built a recording studio in Hollywood. To get things rolling again, Tom took a role in an NBC TV-movie, *Pleasure Cove*. He was well cast as a charming singer with a roguish streak – and a side-line as a smuggler. *Pleasure Cove*, going for the *Fantasy Island* bikinis-and-cocktails market, never made it beyond the pilot, which screened in January 1979. Tom won decent praise, but the flick was instantly forgotten. "I'm not a frustrated actor or anything like that," he pleaded now. "In fact I've always looked on acting as hard work. Now after *Pleasure Cove*, I know that's true." They say family always keep you grounded, and when a cousin said to Tom, "If I was you, I'd stick to singing", he probably heard him.

Nonetheless Tom was pleased to accept a star on the Hollywood Boulevard Walk of Fame.

Years later, with Tom's cool indisputably reaffirmed, there was a happier blockbuster experience. He appeared as himself in 1996's *Mars Attacks!*, director Tim Burton's madcap sci-fi romp. Younger viewers were intrigued by his energy in this manic collision between broad comedy and dark horror. And Tom featured in a stellar cast list, including his friend Jack Nicholson, Glenn Close, Annette Bening, Sarah Jessica Parker, Pierce Brosnan, Rod Steiger, Michael J Fox and others. All Tom really had to do was sing and shimmy as Earth exploded under a Martian invasion. He was a natural.

Memorably, he's performing 'It's Not Unusual' in Vegas when some Martians infiltrate his band. "Jesus Christ!" he exclaims, and bolts backstage. There he joins forces with Annette Bening and boxer Jim Brown. Brown decks a Martian. "Hell of a punch," purrs Tom, admiringly. "Saw you fight in Cardiff, Wales, once." He's then asked to fly a plane, shrugs and heroically does so, and sees Bening to safety. Fortunately Earth is then rescued from certain doom because the Martians don't like the music of Slim Whitman. Tom is one of the few survivors among the wreckage. As the film fades out, we see him standing atop a clifftop, an eagle in one hand, a baby deer held by his other. He's the last man standing, and the intro to 'It's Not Unusual' strikes up. He gets into the groove. End of film. Rebirth of Tom Jones as an icon.

The cool was only slightly rattled in 1998 when, shooting a cameo in Dublin for Anjelica Huston's film *The Mammy*, he kept fluffing his lines. "It's these teeth," he quipped. "They keep falling out."

LEFT: Tom and Cher: Tom was already a master of the celebrity duets scene.

NEXT PAGES: Tom in action... and relaxing with a pint.

If Tom's teeth weren't what they were, one strange phenomenon remained constant throughout the bulk of his career. Since the early days, knickers had been thrown onstage during his gigs. It became a self-perpetuating tradition, a running joke. No matter how often he protested in later times that he was more mature and dignified now and would prefer audiences to listen more seriously to the music, the pants just kept on coming, despite the best efforts of new management to make him more 'cool'. Hysterical female fans just wouldn't let the matter drop.

According to Tom, the custom began in the mid-Sixties at New York's Copacabana club. It then escalated, no doubt encouraged by Mills' PR team, in Vegas. Interviewed by the *Daily Mirror* in '66, Jones hinted at why the ladies got so flushed, when he said, "I'm trying to get across that I'm alive when I sing – the emotion, the sex, the power, the heartbeat, the bloodstream, all of it. The words don't mean as much unless the body gets into the act. Al Jolson got on his knees! Danny Kaye makes with the hips. All the best coloured singers move, man, move! I admit I shove it a bit but I don't spell it out like P.J. Proby." He was tagged "obscene" by some in Australia for taking off his shirt onstage, "because it was bloody hot." In Brisbane a police officer marched into his dressing room

BELOW LEFT: Shaking hands with his good friend Elvis.

BELOW RIGHT: Always giving it 100% on duty.

OPPOSITE: Birthday celebrations. Guests include Joan Rivers, Sonny Bono, Dionne Warwick and Liberace.

NEXT PAGES: This is Tom Jones proved to be successful on both sides of the Atlantic.

and gave him a warning, poking the singer in the chest. "I felt like butting him with the nut but my hair had just been combed for the act." In '83 Jones said, "I like to think I'm a normal, healthy, red-blooded man who doesn't take drugs and who isn't bent. So what I do onstage is exactly how I feel; it's not a false image."

Talking to Chrissy Iley for the *Daily Mail* six years later, he went further. "It's the closest thing to sex that I do. The adoration from the fans is very sexual. My ego needs it: I thrive on it. My biggest fear is that someone will stop me. I have dreams where I'm locked up and have to murder someone to get free. Anything not to be locked up! After my show I dive in the shower and feel like I've performed some great sexual act. I don't think I've got to where I am today without being attractive to women." He'd earlier told the same paper, "It's like foreplay in sex, rather than just jumping on somebody. I've learned

what works by trial and error. The women get excited, I perspire a lot. I used to be self-conscious about it but women handed me their hankies to wipe my brow and then wanted them back. So it just became part of the act." Except it wasn't always hankies.

He was more up for seeing the funny side of things soon afterwards when he told *The Sun*, "I got mobbed the other day. I thought that was (now) reserved for Duran Duran and George Michael! I can't believe they're doing it for an old-timer like me. The fantastic thing is that on *Top of the Pops* they used to think I was the outrageous one, with tight trousers and unbuttoned shirts. That was considered suggestive. Now I'm the traditional one!" And now when knickers landed onstage, he'd hold them up and quip to his band, "Party tonight, lads!" before throwing them back. When fans would yell out that they wanted to have his child, he'd usher Mark

> *" I'm not as pure as the driven snow, but I'm not as naughty as the papers say…I don't want to become a caricature of myself. I know I still have a great voice – so I want to compete. "*

forward and say, "Take him! Here he is!" The comic Eddie Izzard, stepping onstage to introduce Tom at the Albert Hall in '99, could only mutter, "Knickers. And, er, knickers. Knickers everywhere."

After Mark Woodward took charge and reinvented his father's popular image, his wife Donna pushed for the knicker-hurling to stop. Tom obediently told the press, "The underwear has always been the focus in reviews, so Donna said we should get the point across that we don't want it to happen any more." Then he conceded, "But you can't stop something that's been happening for 30 years. I don't think I want it to stop anyway, as long as it doesn't interfere with the show. If you're singing sexy songs to get a sexy reaction, then this is it." He was happy to meet Donna halfway. "I used to use them as props, and think it was all a bit of fun. Then I realised it was getting a bit tacky. The women might still throw them, but I won't pick them up any more." Pressed on the point as to whether he'd accept them if offered, he declared that he would if the donor was very persistent. "It's difficult then – you don't want to seem ungrateful." American actress Brooke Shields, at the time married to tennis star Andre Agassi, once famously enjoyed a Tom Jones concert with great gusto. "I had to scream," she told a US TV show. "I ran up onstage and started dancing with him, but because of the lighting the security people couldn't see who I was and tried to get me down. Maybe I shouldn't have reacted by getting carried away and waving my knickers in the air. I knew that was a bad idea."

To interviewer Martyn Harris, Tom confessed, "I'm not as pure as the driven snow, but I'm not as naughty as the papers say. A husband came up to me after a show once and said: Hey Tom, you pump up the tyres, but it's me that gets to ride the bike."

Tom was, almost despite himself, embracing a level of maturity. "Now, although it's a sexy act, I don't take myself seriously as a sex object," he'd said in '91 before a long UK tour. "A lot of young women come to my shows, but you can look at somebody older and think they're sexy without wanting to go to bed with them. I don't feel fifty-two: only when I look in the mirror am I reminded I'm no longer 30…

"I'm not saying give in to age; I'm just saying that I want to do my best and do it gracefully. I don't mind taking the piss out of myself, but I don't want to become a caricature of myself. I know I still have a great voice – so I want to compete.

"I was never tempted to leave my wife," mused Tom. "We may have homes in two countries but we're usually in one of them together, when I'm not touring." He was touring a lot. "I'd be lying if I said my head wasn't ever turned by some great-looking bird, but then someone might be young and beautiful on the outside…but what is she on the inside? When we married, my wife was 16 and I was 17, and we were inseparable. They were the best times. But youth isn't everything."

Time brings harsh reminders of mortality to all. On August 5, 1986, Tom Jones was a coffin-bearer at the funeral of Gordon Mills, who had died aged just 51. He and Mills had effectively gone from rags to riches together, from the Rhondda Valley villages to the glittering peaks of Hollywood. Former bus conductor Gordon's acumen and Tom's talent had taken them there. Once at the top they'd shared businesses, a determination to stay there, and lavish lifestyles which had been unthinkable in their youth. Now Gordon was gone, not yet old. Tom visited the UK for the first time in three years for the funeral, flying from New York by Concorde then continuing to Hersham, Surrey in a Rolls-Royce. He bade a sad and fond farewell to the Svengali who'd made him one of the entertainment world's biggest stars. His eyes covered by sunglasses, he reflected, "I wasn't just

OPPOSITE: The epitome of 1970s manliness.

close to him. He was as near to me as a brother, my dear friend, my adviser, a big part of my life. He took care of my life."

It was only a month since Gordon had been in a Los Angeles recording studio with Tom and complained of stomach pains. In hospital soon afterwards he was diagnosed with cancer, and his condition swiftly grew worse. Tom went to see him in Cedars Sinai, and said of his last visit: "He didn't look himself. He was no longer there. When I (optimistically) told him his chances were fifty-fifty when he asked me, he said, that's not bad. But there was no hope. He was dying in front of me. I just wanted to pick him up and take him home. He was gone the next day." The interview ended abruptly as Tom was overcome with emotion. Another friend remarked, "Gordon lived fast. He was supposed to go out in a 200 mph car crash…"

On the day of the funeral Tom told the *Daily Mail*, "When we met in Wales, he said that I should be in London making records. Now it wasn't the first time I'd heard that, but the difference was that Gordon actually did something about it. He taught me just about everything. Groomed me, taught me pacing. He tried to be me sitting in the audience watching myself, told me how I would criticise myself. He'd guide me to become larger than life. There are parts of me which he created, totally. We were much more than brothers. As we were both very Welsh, we could get very vocal with each other at times, but we'd always get it straightened out."

As one of the most powerful, influential men in the showbiz industry, Mills was hailed as a kingmaker. Obituaries described his movie-star looks and charisma. A brief (and hated) spell in the army, which taught him self-discipline. The fact that at one time he owned the largest private collection of orang-utans in the world. That he'd also made a star of Jerry Dorsey, who'd asked him for "the Tom Jones treatment" and been re-named Engelbert Humperdinck and given the hit 'Release Me'. That he'd kick-started the career of Raymond O'Sullivan – as Gilbert O'Sullivan – who had even penned a hit ('Clair') inspired by Mills' young daughter.

Asked about his macho persona in 1989, Jones protested, "No, no…I've been upset and faced it. When my father died. When Gordon Mills died. He was like a blood brother." It had been Mills' own musical talent which had given Tom his first big break, of course. "As he co-wrote 'It's Not Unusual', it nearly chokes me to perform it even now."

So how would Tom's career be affected now? It wasn't enjoying its golden period any longer, as styles and tastes evolved in the Eighties. Who could step up to revive the flame and reinvigorate the brand name of Tom Jones?

RIGHT: *Wales, the Land of Song, also known for its rugby.*

For too long Tom had been treading water, perhaps growing complacent…he was in danger of being left behind. Mark knew he had to focus on what made him great…

One young man had been on tour frequently with Jones, observing, learning. Tom's son, Mark Woodward, now aged 29, was full of ideas and recognised it was time to get actively involved. Despite some saying he was generally shy, he rolled up his sleeves and told his dad exactly what he believed needed to be changed and to what ends. Mills had tried to educate him about management, but most accounts claim the two were never close. Mark initiated a watershed, a turn-around, in his father's professional fortunes. This was necessary.

For too long Tom had been treading water, perhaps growing complacent. He'd become, over 18 years, "too Vegas". He was in danger of being left behind as a nostalgia act. He hadn't had a British hit for a long while, and was stuck serving out a dull, going-nowhere-fast six-album deal with the country-music wing of Polygram in America. Mark knew he had to trim the excess fat from Tom's presentation and focus on what made him great, his ability to make a pop song or potent ballad punch above its weight. And so it was with one of each that Tom Jones roared back into the British charts.

4
THE COMEBACK KING

Before 'Kiss', there was the serenade. 'The Boy From Nowhere', a big, old-school ballad, was hardly the flash, modern, futuristic sound of the Eighties, but it served a purpose, re-introducing the long-absent name of Tom Jones to British audiences in 1987. It was taken from the musical *Matador* (based on the life of bullfighter El Cordobes): Tom was tipped to take the leading role when it opened in London's West End, but the show never reached that stage and was shelved at the dissatisfied bullfighter's request. Still, as a rags-to-riches tale the song suited Tom's saccharin side. It also helped to grease the path of transition for his loyal diehard fans, who had a surprise or two coming their way. Not least that this was his first hit of any real size for 14 years.

"It's bloody amazing," Tom told *The Sun*. "I can't remember the last time I got such a reaction. And from young kids too! I'm even getting requests for interviews from trendy music papers. And I'm told that all the Northern Soul clubs are playing 'It's Not Unusual' again…" Clearly Tom had been briefed in bullet-points by new manager and long-term son Mark. There were still a few kinks to be ironed out in his concept of fashion. "I don't spend my whole life in tuxedos, you know. I wear denims too. I still know what young audiences want."

Tom's image had undergone a refurbishment. The Seventies frills and flares had to go, a haircut was in order. There was even a stab at a kind of 'warm leatherette' look, almost a little Gary Numan. It hasn't aged well but was 'in' at the time. Mark axed some musicians from Tom's ensemble and brought in fresher, more topical sounds. He played his dad contemporary music, songs by INXS and, most notably, Prince. When Tom heard Prince's 'Kiss', with its suggestive lyric and hot-funk staccato rhythm, he cottoned on to the appeal, bringing it into his live set. The song was to take his career onto the next level. "I wanted to put more meat into it than he had."

His cover of 'Kiss' raced into the Top Ten after a performance on Jonathan Ross' TV show *The Last Resort*. Ross and his producers had said, with due honesty, that they'd prefer the singer to do something a tad more upbeat and youth-oriented for their hip audience than 'The Boy From Nowhere'. Ross was a fan of 'Kiss' and Tom said, "We'll do that then!" He did it with dazzling verve, swagger and commitment and the show was a much-discussed 'water-cooler moment', spawning the hit single. Tom Jones was back! "Success is the best revenge", he winked.

As he remarked to the *Mail On Sunday*, "I know what people were saying about me – he 'used' to make good records. Now I can put all that to rest and show what I can do again, it's great. My hands were tied with the Polygram country music division, but since Mark made me listen to 'Kiss', it's been a turning-point. After one hit, you look for more."

The man himself couldn't really understand why people were so stunned at his electric onscreen energy. To his mind he wasn't doing very much different to what he'd always done – though possibly in cooler settings and an arguably better wardrobe. "Weird," he mused. "I'm always doing stuff like that in my stage show, but if people don't come to see it they don't know. I haven't recorded anything like this for years though…" Mark had by now extricated his father from the stagnating American record deal and signed him to Jive Records, a popular soul-and-rap-based label in the UK. A cleverly voguish video for 'Kiss' had him decked out in an 'ironic' over-large suit. "A hot, contemporary album" (long overdue in career terms) was promised.

With allies like The Art of Noise, this seemed plausible. Anne Dudley and J.J. Jeczalik of the critically-acclaimed ZTT studio outfit were among those who saw Tom perform 'Kiss' on TV. They'd recently taken to reviving under-appreciated careers, like that of guitar hero Duane Eddy. Mark was keen when they got in touch. Tom said, with no false modesty, "They laid down a track in London and sent it to me in LA, where I added the vocals. When they heard how powerful the voice was, they reworked the track to complement it. It's become a first-class production." And now, with 'Kiss' also a hit in America, credible producers were queuing up to get involved with that ever-powerful voice. Producers such as Timmy Allen, who'd worked with Millie Jackson and Stephanie Mills, and Barry Eastmond, who'd given Billy Ocean a second lease of pop life. Somewhat disappointingly, the subsequent album – named after its title track 'Move Closer' (an interpretation of the recent Phyllis Nelson chart-topper) – didn't set the charts alight. It peaked at number 34. Yet Tom Jones was very much on the map again.

The managed-by-Mark-Woodward era was off to a flying start. What Tom Jones' son saw as dead wood from the Gordon Mills years had been chopped away. He further reminded the public of his father's pop stature by ensuring that a 1987 re-release of 'It's Not Unusual' revisited the top twenty. Tom was on *Top of the Pops* again.

> " *Jones discussed his re-found mojo.* "
> *"I'm hip again, there's a buzz about me," he acknowledged.*

Tom, naturally, sang his son's praises. "We've always been close. He's been on the road with me since he was 17. We're very alike." Both father and son, it's been said, still enjoyed a few drinks. When Tom happily visited a Pontypridd pub around Christmas time in '88, he smiled, "Girls were coming up for my autograph and raving about 'Kiss', saying I did it better than Prince. But the fellas in the pub I went to school with were saying, that's all right, but 'The Boy From Nowhere' is you, that's who you are." He told *The Times*, "There are two completely different groups that both, thank God, like what I do." The danger however was of falling between two stools by trying to appease both camps. Mark was eager not to allow that to happen. He maintained that Tom's act must be streamlined, refined, to woo the younger generation.

1989 saw Tom picking up an MTV Video Music Award. Now all Mark had to do was guide Tom's career out of the Eighties and into a whole new decade. The star was reassessed and rehabilitated by critics, the fallow years of ill-advised country music left behind him. Ahead lay inspired collaborations and a respect that mixed knowing irony and genuine awe to a healthy degree. In 1989 in the *Guardian*, a panting Caroline Sullivan reviewed his Hammersmith Odeon show thus: "Tom Jones is a risible Las Vegas hack with no relevance to contemporary music? Wrong! If you have ever thrilled to pop music, you would have been Watusiing in the aisles during this gig. He doesn't so much dance as occasionally stop short to briefly rotate his pelvis in the lewdest manner possible. And there are more than a few hungry-eyed teenage lovelettes in the front rows, all speculating on the source of the outlandish convexity at the front of his black jeans. I found myself at the foot of the stage, brandishing a hankie, with about fifteen other women…" Even the *NME* reckoned, "Concealed inside that frame is one of the most powerful voices known to nature." And in the hippest magazine of the era, *Melody*

Maker, Kris Kirk wrote, "Fads may come and fads may go, but true quality never wanes. The man is the best rock'n'roll voice Britain ever produced, Billy Fury included." Mary Kemp in *The People* was echoing Sullivan's lust in 1991 when reporting, "His eyes just follow every movement you make, taking in the way you smooth your skirt or drink your coffee. He certainly makes you feel good, as if you're the most beautiful girl in the world."

Jones displayed some self-awareness discussing his re-found mojo. "I'm hip again; there's a buzz about me again," he acknowledged. He then added, "I know I'm not ugly, but I'm not handsome either. Yet I think I must be attractive. When people tell you that all the time, it rubs off on you." His tastes in music seemed upgraded and rebooted for the times too. He praised Madonna as "a girl who's got everything. She can sing, dance, and hold a crowd in her hand." He rated George Michael as "a great songwriter and an excellent live singer with plenty of staying power." Of Boy George, he declared, "Now he's stopped wearing all his crazy clothes, you can see the talent clearly." He was less kind to some of those closer to his own age group, however, and was reported to have sniffed that Cliff Richard was "mild, like going through life on tranquillisers" and that Mick Jagger "knows he doesn't have a good voice so he does the best with the tools he has." He was particularly harsh to Phil Collins ("he makes a monotonous sound with no sex or warmth") and said more generally of his competitors, "I don't understand how they do so well… especially with the women."

Eyebrows were raised, then, when it was announced that his next album was to be a collaboration with Van Morrison. *"Carrying A Torch"* was a surprising next move for Tom. After Mark had so successfully re-branded his dad as an evergreen king of cool, Van was hardly a sleek and cutting-edge pop act. What he did have was long-held credibility, so that perhaps explains the appeal of the slightly retrogressive venture to the Jones camp.

OPPOSITE: *A brief flirtation with the 'warm leatherette' look.*

Belfast-born Morrison wrote and produced half the album. The title song sneaked into the lower end of the singles chart. Upon release, Tom dutifully talked the album up to *The Times*. "I've always had that problem of finding the right material, especially nowadays. Most writers are performers and do their own songs, so it's hard to get first crack at it. For me, it's like the difference between actors and scriptwriters. I find it easy to put over a good song, but I can't write. So when Van came over with these songs for me to listen to, I thought: how the hell do you come up with these things?"

Yet *Carrying A Torch* failed to fire the popular imagination, selling poorly. It reached number 44. Tom admitted to more honest doubts when speaking to Adam Sweeting for *The Guardian* in 1994. "It was definitely Van Morrison music, which is fine, but after doing stuff like 'Kiss' I'd wanted to do more like that."

Had he blown his chance at image-reinvention? He had not, such was the public's affection for him. Mark

continued to put him in front of more current audiences. For Comic Relief he was paired with comic Lenny Henry, in his guise as mock sex-god singer Theophilus P. Wildebeest, as both sent themselves up. "I've always said I don't take myself too seriously," said Tom, wearing for the televised skit a giant codpiece from which burst forth a flashing red nose. He was joining in with the more highbrow animated humour of US show *The Simpsons* (where all the writers professed to be Tom Jones fans) in '92. An entire episode revolved around Marge Simpson's love of guest star Tom. Marge requests that the nuclear power plant at which she works alongside dopey husband Homer boost staff morale by piping in the music of Jones The Voice. 'What's New Pussycat?' fills the Springfield airwaves. Tom is kidnapped and chained to a radiator by evil Mr Burns, then offered to Marge in an attempt at seduction. All ends happily.

Tom persisted, under Mark's guidance, in taking risks with edgier material and hook-ups. He was still playing

---

PREVIOUS PAGES: *Still the consummate ladies' man.*

ABOVE: *A trip to Harrods with former owner Mohamed Al-Fayed.*

OPPOSITE: *A guest appearance on* The Fresh Prince of Bel-Air *with Will Smith.*

NEXT PAGES: *Tom tried out a few wardrobe changes during this period.*

" *I'm not just in one area of music, and never have been.* "
I want to see something in print about my voice for a change!

Vegas (to great financial gain), but this led to a memorable cameo. He guested on *Sandra After Dark*, an American TV special helmed by provocative singer-comedienne-actress Sandra Bernhard, an avowed Tom fanatic who'd witnessed his Vegas act. As the unlikely pair duetted on a cover of the EMF hit 'Unbelievable', Bernhard dropped to the ground beneath Tom to simulate an R-rated act, her microphone between her legs. Said a suddenly prim Tom, "I just looked at her, like, what are you doing down there? She's nuts! She didn't do any of that in rehearsal!" Bernhard smiled, "He's such a pro. And he hasn't lost his sex appeal."

Bruce Willis was another Hollywood star happy to link up with the Welshman. Tom sang at the actor's fortieth birthday party, at his request. Willis owned the Idaho club in which the party took place, and fulfilled an ambition by joining Tom for an encore of 'Great Balls Of Fire'. "I did get to sing with him," smiled Willis, "but only because I owned the night club!" Tom returned the mutual affection. Sort of. "He's good. He hasn't got a great vocal range, but he has a great attitude and he knows his R&B." The friendship was maintained, as the following year Bruce and then-wife Demi Moore visited Jones backstage after his Wembley Arena show. That night they'd sat next to another fan: Sarah Ferguson, Duchess of York.

Younger stars were now coming out as Tom Jones fans too. Tom was seen on key shows like those of David Letterman and Jay Leno, and memorably made a guest appearance on *The Fresh Prince Of Bel Air*, the sitcom serving as a vehicle for soon-to-be-stellar Will Smith. Luke Perry and Jason Priestley wanted him to appear on their show *Beverly Hills 90210*. That didn't happen but the three met up in California, with Perry saying, "It was great having the chance to spend time with Tom. If my mom knew, she'd go crazy!" Tom laughed good-naturedly, "Their mothers had all my records. It turned out they really did know my work. Not just the hits." When the rising heart-throbs asked him

how best to handle the ladies, they were sagely told, "Be yourself – and be careful."

With all this TV exposure and the revived demand for Tom's charisma, it seemed to him and to Mark that perhaps he should try hosting his own show again. It was the right time. Or was it? Nobody had the budget to match the classic old Tom telly shows of the Seventies, yet elements of the format decided upon weren't too dissimilar. Tom hosted and sang alongside or chatted to guests from a wide range of musical styles and periods, who'd cover a song that had inspired them and discuss their influences. Named after a favourite Ray Charles song (thankfully, as Tom had also joked it was to be called, less classily, *Keep Your Knickers On*), the six-part series *The Right Time* was shot in Nottingham and saw appearances from an eclectic list: from Stevie Wonder, Daryl Hall and Al Jarreau to Lyle Lovett, Erasure and Shakespear's Sister. The range indicated that Tom's aim, ideally, was to trace the evolution of pop music from roots to radicals, no less. He told the *Daily Telegraph* he wanted to "explain where pop music came from". Channel 4 screened the Central TV shows and sold them on to America.

"I'm not just in one area of music, and never have been," he offered. "They said I could do whatever I wanted…and I want to see something in print about my voice for a change. It'll cover the development of pop music from the turn of the century to present-day funk, metal and rap. It's going to be great fun." Although Tom came across as a genuinely interested and knowledgeable host, it's debatable whether the show really captured his strengths. Critics opined that it fell between chat show and music show. The first in the series saw EMF playing 'Unbelievable' (now a staple in Tom's own set), Erasure covering Abba's 'S.O.S.', Marianne Faithfull singing 'The Ballad of Lucy Jordan' and Shakespear's Sister taking a stab at T.Rex's 'Hot Love'. Jones himself put the cherry on top with typically emphatic versions of the Beatles' 'Come Together' and Bruce Springsteen's 'Dancing In The

OPPOSITE: A few flecks of silver only enhance Tom's roguish charm.

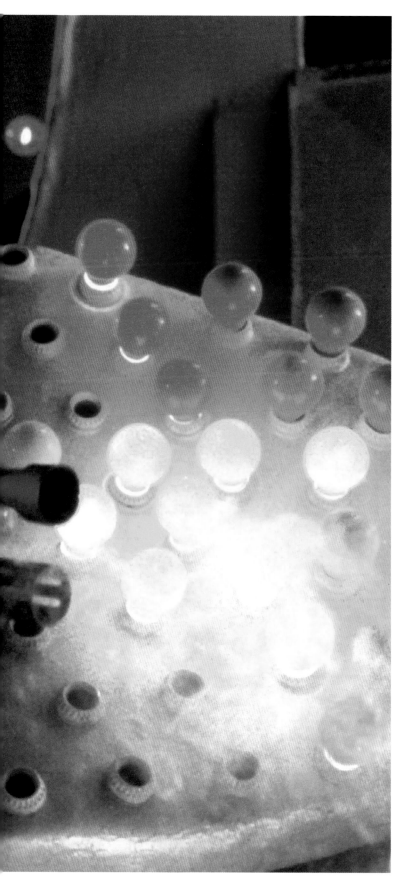

Dark'. Following shows offered, among others, Joe Cocker, Pops Staples, Cyndi Lauper and Mica Paris. "It's a chance to do the stuff I've always wanted to do," announced Tom, pitching his versatility. "Gospel, blues, soul; even Celtic music. I've been seen as a narrow balladeer, but what I like are performers with big strong straightforward songs. Some are right over the top. Just like me!"

Another profile boost arrived when the prestigious BBC arts show *Omnibus* dedicated a Good Friday special to Jones in 1991. "Singing is my hobby", he told the cameras. "Most people look forward to retiring so they can devote time to their hobby, but I'll keep on doing this until I can't. I dread that day. I'm glad to be here. Elvis was only forty-two when he died. For me the kick is still there and it's a tremendous feeling." He added that he could still perform a two-hour show with "ease", although two shows a night was tricky now. He hadn't always been so wisely cautious. Recalling sharing a bill with the Rolling Stones, he reckoned he hadn't done anything too different to Mick Jagger except that Jagger "camped it up a bit more. But maybe I seemed a bit more real, and that scared some of the girls…"

Of course in more recent times Tom Jones has come back to dominate Saturday night's primetime schedules on British television, displaying his knowledge and acumen on *The Voice*. In the early Nineties though, he was still seeking the perfect vehicle, and trying to make an indisputably fine album. Again, his next move was one that few saw coming.

In 1993 Tom signed a new recording deal with Interscope, a credible cutting-edge label part-run by Janet Jackson's mentor John McClain, and whose roster included Dr Dre, Snoop Dogg and Nine Inch Nails. Not only did Tom go as far out as these left-field acts, nobly refusing to grow old gracefully; many reckoned he over-compensated and went too far. The ensuing album was certainly a brave, intriguing affair, and although it barely nudged the top fifty in the UK, it sold forty thousand copies within its first fortnight of release. Oddly, it went to number one in Finland. It was, all round, very odd.

The Lead And How To Swing It, released in 1994 (on ZTT in the UK), remains unique among Tom's canon, and not just for that title. Diverse big-name producers worked on it, like Jeff Lynne, Teddy Riley, Trevor Horn, Flood and Youth, and Tom duetted with Tori Amos and collaborated with avant-garde arthouse acts like The Wolfgang Press and DJ Battlecat. And yet he did this while revealing a new image. "Whether he revels in the irony or is oblivious to it isn't entirely clear", wrote Adam Sweeting in the *Guardian*. He deduced that, "a man prepared to dress in a string vest and Sta-Prest trousers on the front of his album sleeve and a red PVC suit on the back is either doing it for a bet or has a

LEFT: Tom and Annette Bening try to save the planet in the Tim Burton movie Mars Attacks!

great sense of humour." Overall he was sceptical: "Who can say whether the joke's on us for taking Jones' bizarre stylistic gyrations seriously, or on him for deluding himself that a 54-year-old veteran of Vegas and the cabaret circuit could possibly be a contender in the era of ambient dub and the internet?" Jones was still getting people talking, that much was undeniable. Another reinvention and re-boot.

The image perhaps detracted from the serious intent of the challenging music. The Producer Youth declared that, "His power and passion and delivery remain unchallenged in contemporary pop music", while The Wolfgang Press said of their unlikely new friend, "What Tom has that others today do not is soul and sex." Soon Tom was working with New Model Army, and almost collaborated on a musical with Malcolm McLaren.

He was being taken seriously enough for US magazine *Entertainment Weekly* to shout: "He's Mister Retro-Cool! Once again, Tom Jones is hot!" He shared the bill with Sting, Tina Turner, Bryan Adams and George Michael at a rainforest benefit concert at Carnegie Hall in New York. Esteemed writer and soul expert Gerri Hershey reckoned that "only Tina Turner matched him for lung power and locomotion." Meanwhile, rather more frivolously, notorious radio shock-jock Howard Stern was announcing on air to Jones that, "I think the reason women used to throw panties at you was because you have a big package in your pants. It's for real: it's not like you stuffed socks in there." Tim concurred that he never did that. He confessed that he had occasionally taken young models to his hotel for "a drink". Stern summarised thus: "You're a Welshman. And Welshmen are horny." The Welshman was still dividing his time between America and Britain and still selling out Vegas or Wembley whenever he chose to play.

At the 1994 MTV Music Awards in Berlin, Tom appeared along with such luminaries as George Michael, Take That and Björk. *Rolling Stone* acclaimed "the magic of Tom Jones". Even 'indie guru' DJ John Peel raved, "I never believed I'd be jumping up and down shouting for 'Delilah', but when I saw Tom Jones perform he was wonderful." Indeed his performance at the Glastonbury festival was exhilarating enough to win over those among the young generation not already comprehensively wooed. Tom's recollection afterwards was that he'd seen thousands of unwashed indie youths rushing en masse towards the stage as he opened his set, and wasn't sure what to think. Then he saw a home-made banner, too big to miss, being unfurled. He approved of it. "It read: 'Tom Fucking Jones!' That's me, all right – Tom Fucking Jones!" He laughed, "Wouldn't it be great to use that all the time?"

OPPOSITE: It's hard to imagine this man working with post-punk bands like The Wolfgang Press and New Model Army.

RIGHT: A suited and booted Tom contemplates the appropriate height for his waistband.

" '*He's Mister Retro-Cool! Once again Tom Jones is magazine* Entertainment *hot!' shouted US Weekly."*

5
RELOAD

For all this fresh momentum, Tom's career now entered a couple of relatively quiet years. Whatever scheming and plotting went on in that time paid rich dividends, as his next album, *Reload*, was to rocket him back to the top of the charts in 1999.

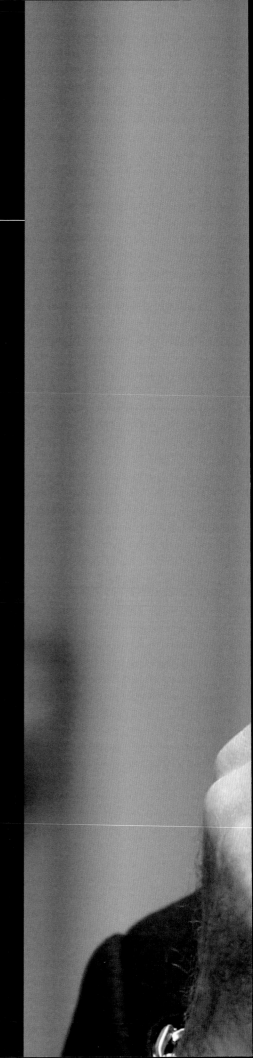

"Relatively quiet" was in fact busy by most standards. Tom kept himself in the limelight with a Christmas TV special in 1996, entitled *Tom Jones – For One Night Only*. He gave the fans hits like 'It's Not Unusual' and 'Delilah' but also offered some unexpected treats. He duetted with a range of stars from Welsh opera singer Bryn Terfel to soul queen Toni Braxton. Mark Knopfler, once of Dire Straits, also appeared. "My voice has more weight to it now," said Tom. "There's an edge to it that comes…just from having lived longer. After you've been around a bit, you can put more into a lyric because you read more into it…"

As a limber-up to another mother of all comebacks, 1997 saw him starring on the soundtrack to the British film and runaway hit *The Full Monty*. His version of 'You Can Leave Your Hat On' perfectly complemented the story's nudge-wink male-strippers appeal. It became very popular and led to his unforgettable duet with Robbie Williams, then as hot as hot gets in the UK, at the 1998 BRIT Awards. The announcement was made that Tom and the former Take That star were to blast out a medley of songs, including 'You Can Leave Your Hat On', the Wilson Pickett soul classic 'Land Of 1,000 Dances' (an old Tom favourite) and the Steve Harley & Cockney Rebel Seventies hit, '(Come Up And See Me) Make Me Smile'. Robbie spoke of Tom as his idol. "I'm going to do a duet with the mighty Tom Jones!" he exclaimed. "He's my hero!" Added a Brit Awards spokesman, "It's the icing on the cake – two generations coming together on songs from a great British film." The film hasn't stood the test of time, but Tom already had. After the performance, most critics rated him as the cooler of the not-very-shy pair, though Tom was magnanimous. "I think (Robbie) is great. I get off on the respect of young performers."

Surely the most hilarious reaction came from the man who told his "story" to The *Sun*. Mitch Charles, of Ilford, Essex, complained that the way Tom "jiggled his hips" caused his television to explode. "The second he jumped onstage and gyrated…there was a big bang and smoke started pouring out of the back of it and the picture went dead…" The man reckoned "Tom's got millions – more than enough money to buy us a nice plush telly with a remote control."

Tom survived this anecdote to play in front of around 100,000 spectators at the Party In The Park organised by the Prince's Trust in July at Hyde Park, London. His set featured 'You Can Leave Your Hat On' and 'Delilah' and he stole the Stephen Fry-compered show from a line-up including Lionel Richie, Boyzone, Gary Barlow, Shania Twain, The Corrs and All Saints. In her review, Victoria Coren (now best known as the host of TV show *Only Connect*), declared, "He may be 58, he may have teenage grandchildren – but Tom Jones is still the undisputed champion of the world. He's the sultan of sex, the baron of ballads, the ruler of rock. When he took to the stage, one can only hope Prince Charles felt obliged to make a respectful bow." A happy Tom admitted he was partying backstage afterwards till five in the morning – "as usual. Could have been six." Only Boyzone kept up with him, he said. "They're good lads. They enjoy a drink."

Tom and wife Linda were now dividing their time equally between a new house in LA and Wales. The mansion Tom had inhabited after Dean Martin was now sold to film actor Nicolas Cage. And even if the famously diplomatic Duke of Edinburgh was likening Tom's singing style to "gargling in gravel", others rather younger than Prince Philip were singing his praises. Some literally, rather than figuratively. Not content with being an icon, he became a character in a hit song. In March 1998, the band Space, with guest vocals by Cerys Matthews of Welsh group Catatonia, released 'The Ballad of Tom Jones', which went on to be a sizeable top three hit. The song told a narrative of a warring couple who fight over everything but resolve their grievances by enjoying Tom's greatest hits together. In an unscripted twist, Space's lead singer's name was… Tommy Scott. Tom had of course been very familiar with that name in his younger years.

As for that "gargling in gravel" comment from a member of the royal family, Tom's reply was a calm "I must be doing something right then." The Duke did later apologise, anyway. Tom himself was prone to saying the odd dodgy thing. Asked about the tabloids' scandal stories still linking him with young women, he blurted, "At least it's natural stuff. I mean, nobody's suggesting I had sex with kids or anything. Or sheep." The less said about that gaffe the better, perhaps. He was on safer ground waxing melancholy about the acting career which never took off. "You can't turn the clock back, but I wonder what would have happened if I'd done more acting earlier. All men are boys at heart – I'd love to have done a Western, on a horse with a gun on my hip."

It was definitely time to reload.

"Tom has a remarkable ability to reinvent himself for each succeeding generation. We know the esteem in which he's held by stars who weren't even born when Tom made his first records." So said Guy Holmes, then chairman of Gut Records, who along with Tom's son Mark took executive producer credits for the album which consolidated and defined the next phase of Jones' career. *Reload* – a set of well-chosen collaborations and duets with a broad spectrum of the time's biggest names in rock and pop – saw him exit the twentieth century on a dazzling, chart-topping high.

"After the BRIT Awards appearance with Robbie, kids kept coming up to me and asking who I was going to work with next," Tom stated before recordings got under way. "I thought: let's go for it. It would have been boring just to bash out old stuff like 'Delilah' again. I'm flattered that these younger bands want to sing with me, and these are all songs that none of us have ever done before." No stranger to the art of the duet, he warmed to his theme, adding, "I've had some of the best times singing with other singers and bands, throughout my career. So I'm very pleased that these artists have said yes to the invitation, because I'm sure something very special is going to happen when we get down to working together. Every single one of them is fresh and strong, no matter what kind of music they do or how long they've been around. I am absolutely thrilled to be having this experience."

The album of 15 cover versions and two originals was recorded in the individual studios which most of the collaborating artists normally used, with their producer, so as to ensure they had the best chance of transmitting their sound and style. The gambit worked spectacularly, with *Reload*, released on 16 September, 1999 on Gut Records through V2, reaching number one for a week in October – and then reclaiming the top spot in May and June of 2000 as its hit singles relit its fire. It could thus (depending on your knack for dates) be said to be both Tom's last number one of one century and his first of another. It was his highest-selling album to date and sold over six million copies worldwide. It went four times platinum in the UK and double platinum in Australia and Italy. (If the master strategy had an Achilles' heel, it was in the States, where many of the fashionable young British bands weren't well-known).

The biggest hit single turned out to be one of the two originals (the other was 'Looking Out My Window' with the James Taylor Quartet): 'Sex Bomb', with Mousse T, took up residence in the UK top three, and has become a crowd-pleasing staple of Tom's set since, not to mention a cheesy dance-floor favourite. It

OPPOSITE: Re-loaded and re-laundered.

RIGHT: Tom receives his star on the Hollywood Walk of Fame.

simultaneously celebrated and lampooned Tom's long-standing public image.

Other stand-out tracks ranged from duets with the perkily up-and-coming to some with more gnarled veterans. So it leapt from a version of INXS's 'Never Tear Us Apart' with Aussie songbird Natalie Imbruglia to another effort ('Sometimes We Cry') with previous collaborator Van Morrison. Said Imbruglia, "I kept thinking, my God, that's Tom Jones…and I'm singing with him! I was so excited that I kept forgetting to do my bit!" Talking Heads' 'Burning Down The House' was recorded with The Cardigans, while Randy Newman's 'Mama Told Me Not To Come', once a hit for Three Dog Night, was revisited with Welsh rockers Stereophonics, who became Tom's latest drinking buddies. The Welsh

angle reappeared on the cover of Elvis Presley's 'I'm Left, You're Right, She's Gone' alongside James Dean Bradfield of Manic Street Preachers. Robbie Williams popped up on 'Are You Gonna Go My Way?', the Lenny Kravitz song, while there was a more subtle sound to 'All Mine', a Portishead track with The Divine Comedy. Space, who'd earned their call with 'The Ballad Of Tom Jones', came in for The Kinks' 'Sunny Afternoon', and Heather Small of M-People bellowed along to the Motown classic 'You Need Love Like I Do'. (A version of 'You Can Leave Your Hat On' with All Saints didn't quite make it).

One of the most exciting cuts saw Chrissie Hynde of the Pretenders team up with Tom to take a run through Iggy Pop's 'Lust For Life', while another Welsh

star, Cerys Matthews, joined her idol for an enjoyable romp through Frank Loesser's 'Baby It's Cold Outside'. (The pair memorably stole the show on *Jools Holland's Hootenanny* with this). Filling out the album were a peculiar 'Little Green Bag' with Canada's Barenaked Ladies, 'Ain't That A Lot Of Love' with Simply Red's Mick Hucknall, and Fine Young Cannibals' 'She Drives Me Crazy' with Italian singer Zucchero. As the album's serious finale, Portishead backed Tom on the traditional, mournful ballad 'Motherless Child'. A special edition of the album added remixes of 'You Need Love Like I Do' and of course 'Sex Bomb'.

If there were quite a few miles of mood between 'Sex Bomb' and 'Motherless Child', the public and press didn't seem to mind. *Reload* became a smash, perhaps beyond even the expectations of its makers. Reviews hailed Tom Jones as "as driving and contemporary as ever", with Allmusic describing the album as "ultra-modern and topical…invigorating" and praising the way Tom still took songs of every genre and made them his own.

Could 1999 get any more euphoric and eventful for Tom? It could, as the year saw him awarded an OBE. "Very special", he beamed. By June 2000, when Tom Jones OBE – not so very long ago written-off by some as a has-been – celebrated his sixtieth birthday, with his latest album ubiquitous across the nation, he must

OPPOSITE : The steely blue eyes of a man at the top of his game.

BELOW: Admiring his own handiwork.

> " *Tom spent New Year's Eve – the last night of the century – singing at the 2000 Millennium celebrations in Washington DC, at the personal request of President Bill Clinton.* "

have been a very happy man. And he was still looking forwards, not back.

A few months before the resurrection that was *Reload*, Jones, by now well used to singing at Cardiff Arms Park, was singing the Welsh national anthem (as well as 'Green, Green Grass Of Home' and 'Delilah') at a packed Twickenham Stadium at the Wales versus England rugby international. Suitably motivated, the Welsh went on that 1999 afternoon to beat the English for the first time in years. And the very same weekend, Jones joined a bill featuring *Reload* cast member Chrissie Hynde, Elvis Costello, Johnny Marr and Sinead O'Connor at the Royal Albert Hall for the Linda McCartney memorial concert. Sir Paul McCartney of course headlined. Fittingly, Tom sang the Beatles' 'She's A Woman', then offered a moving 'Green, Green Grass Of Home' with Hynde, O'Connor and Des'ree on accompanying vocals. Another proud-to-be-Welsh moment came when he performed at the Cardiff Castle concert marking the opening of the Welsh Assembly. He then joined other stars on a rousing rendition of Cerys Matthews and Catatonia's new anthem, 'Every Day When I Wake Up, I Thank The Lord I'm Welsh'. The title had become something of a catchphrase, marking a resurgence in Welsh music and more generally national pride around this period. It had been a long while since so many new Welsh bands had enjoyed a broader profile, as Manic Street Preachers, Catatonia, Stereophonics, Super Furry Animals and others were now doing. Tom, still the godfather, welcomed the new kids on the block, gamely joining in with a commercial for the BBC Wales TV channel to recite the above phrase with a big grin.

His fame still stretched far and wide. He spent New Year's Eve – the last night of the century – singing at the 2000 Millennium celebrations in Washington DC, at the personal request of President Bill Clinton, whose fondness for Tom Jones' stage persona makes more sense the more you think about it. In Australia, Tom was asked to sing the commercial to market their 2000 rugby league season,

thus becoming 'the voice of the game' down under. An extraordinary period of career revival was capped by his winning the Best British Male award at the 2000 BRITs, beating much younger competition. Surely nobody could have seen that coming a few years earlier. (Three years later, he took it further, picking up the Outstanding Contribution To Music award.)

His next album didn't arrive until December 2002, and it was another curveball. Again confounding expectations, Tom joined forces with Wyclef Jean, the Haitian rapper/ singer/producer (and latterly politician), who had made his name with popular hip-hop trio Fugees. Their 1996 album *The Score*, blessed with the vocals of Lauryn Hill, had sold over eighteen million copies, spawning the singles 'Killing Me Softly', 'Fu-Gee-La' and 'Ready Or Not'. Wyclef was now one of the hottest, most in-demand producers in the world, and had enjoyed plentiful solo hits. He had also helmed the America: A Tribute To Heroes benefit concert following the terrorist attacks of 11 September, 2001. 2002 had seen the release of this prolific star's third album, *Masquerade*, and a reworking of 'What's New Pussycat?' thereon, named 'Pussycat', boasted one Tom Jones as guest vocalist.

So a Wyclef and Tom team-up had not been on many prediction cards. It showed that Jones was still very much aware of contemporary musical trends, and flagged up Wyclef's diversity. "It's a combination of hip-hop, R&B, and his regular pop sound," declared Wyclef. "I always looked at Tom Jones as being half soul singer." His next comment was less weighty. "He's where I got my 'ladies' man' thing from. Ladies throw their bras at me because of Tom Jones."

Mr. Jones, released on V2, while a bold move, wasn't perhaps an unqualified triumph. Co-produced by Jean and Jerry Duplessis, its dance-based tracks fared much less well than *Reload* commercially. Critics though were

---

OPPOSITE: *Tom Jones – "half soul-singer", according to Wyclef Jean.*

strangely intrigued. As William Ruhlmann wrote, "Aged 62, Tom Jones is, in a sense, making a comeback with each new recording…" Songs were often co-written by the singer and producers, with the bizarre opener 'Tom Jones International' even seeing Tom rap, in a homage to himself. Indeed there were several elements of sketchy autobiography, seemingly mimicking rappers' bravado, as on 'Younger Days', which reflected on past glories before trumpeting that Tom had still got what it takes. Covers included an emphatic rasp of Leadbelly's 'Black Betty' (featuring a sample of its original singer) and a more sedate, conciliatory walk through the Bob Seger romantic ballad 'We've Got Tonight'. The album climaxed in a pretty radical re-working (complete with old Tom Jones samples) of the big-lungs broken-heart standard 'I Who Have Nothing', which Tom had first recorded 32 years earlier. It appeared that the producers had thought the best way to pitch their charge now was to big up his legend with lots of self-referential, almost post-modern, winks. And update the backing beats. When it worked, *Mr. Jones* was smart, sassy stuff. It doesn't always work though, and the choice of producers is open to criticism. Perhaps conservatively, perhaps wisely, Tom's next album was rather a return to basic rock'n'roll roots.

Tom Jones and Jools Holland, released in 2004 on Radar, saw Tom back in the top five of the UK album charts. Holland, once a member of Squeeze, is of course now better-known as an all-round musician and unlikely, bumbling TV host. He is prone – some might say overly so – to collaborating with the stars who appear on his TV show. Tom had appeared on the piano player's *New Year's Eve Special Hootenanny* in 1998 and on its mothership programme *Later* a little, er, later, and they had discovered during rehearsals that they shared a love of certain old blues and rock'n'roll songs. A selection of such favourite chestnuts comprised their album, along with a few self-penned originals.

BBC Wales reported that Tom played the new album to Jerry Lee Lewis, a major influence on the record. "He loved it," said the singer. "He asked how old Jools was and I said he was in his forties. Jerry said, "Tell that boy he can play." Coming from Jerry Lee Lewis, that's amazing. He doesn't like other piano players. He thinks he invented boogie-woogie. So I was knocked out by that." So, naturally, was Jools, who beamed, "Well, I'm so flattered. In fact we had to get the builders over, because my head was so big we had to knock a wall out. One of

---

RIGHT: Mr Jones, working on his new 'dance music' direction.

NEXT PAGES: After contrasting albums with Wyclef Jean and Jools Holland, Tom deserved a drink of water.

my favourite hobbies is boasting down the pub, so I was straight down there with something to boast about."

Both artists had begun their careers playing old-school boogie numbers in pubs and clubs, so the bonding was unforced. Holland said, "At *Later…*we found out we both knew some of these songs, and they sounded so good, so we put them in the show. Then we went out one night and Tom started singing. People were straining to see what was going on. I thought: this is mad, we should make a record!" It took some time as both had other commitments, but once recording started it proceeded apace. "This is material we both loved when we first started doing it," Tom offered. "I heard a lot of these records when they first came out. It's the kind of stuff I started doing in Wales – rock'n'roll, rhythm and blues, soulful ballads." So the album was full of spontaneity, with first takes often used. "We both wanted this album to be recognisably us," said Jools. "We hope that when you hear it, the old songs sound like our reinvention of them, because they're alongside some we've written." "We wanted to keep it light," added Tom. "What we first did in the rehearsal room on Jools' *Hootenanny* show, that's what we wanted to record."

Mixing upbeat numbers like '200 Pounds of Heavenly Joy' with the more mellow 'Glory of Love' and the jazzy 'St. James Infirmary Blues', the album was a showcase for Holland's ivory-tinkling and Jones' complete ease with, and mastery of, the genres. Its fusion of nostalgia and vitality (and a little country) proved more palatable to radio stations and record-buyers than Tom's work with Wyclef, and, while only a success in the UK, was warmly received there. And in its earthiness and stripped-back stylings – a contrast to knicker-throwing and sex bombs – lay the seeds of some acclaimed Tom Jones albums yet to come.

In 2005 the BBC announced that Tom Jones was Wales' wealthiest entertainer, with a personal fortune of £175 million. He had reaped the dividends of career longevity. It was appropriate then that he came back to the land of his fathers to play in Pontypridd, where it all began, for the first time since 1964 (the year before his first hit, 'It's Not Unusual'). A crowd of around twenty thousand saw him belt out the greats in Ynysangharad Park. Taking place on 28 May, the concert effectively celebrated his imminent 65th birthday on the green, green grass of home.

Later that same year he recorded a live album, primarily for the Australian market, with John Farnham. It was called simply *John Farnham & Tom Jones – Together In Concert*. It was swept under the carpet in the UK, where Farnham wasn't exactly a household name, but the next

LEFT: Never afraid to work up a sweat.

year Tom issued a much more 'happening' release in the shape of the dance track 'Stoned In Love', a team-up with Chicane. The single drew positive reviews and reached a healthy number seven in the charts. A comprehensive 23-track Greatest Hits also emerged, ranging all the way from 'It's Not Unusual' to 'Sex Bomb'.

The highlight of his 2006 came in March when the singer, once deemed outrageous and licentious, was knighted by the Queen at Buckingham Palace, just seven years after receiving his OBE. Sir Tom – so dubbed for services to music – was thrilled. "When you first come into show business and have a hit record, it's the start of something," he gushed. "As time goes by it just gets better. But this is the best thing I've had. It's a wonderful feeling, a heady feeling." The man – sorry, the knight – was invested as Thomas Woodward, and went on to call it a "great and humbling honour". He told the BBC afterwards, "It's fantastic. It was lovely to see the Queen again. I love seeing the Queen and have always been a royalist. She is lovely, still lovely. She has a great smile and her whole face lights up when she uses it." This might sound over-familiar, but he had actually first met her as long ago as 1966 at a charity performance. The Queen apparently remembered this, and asked exactly how many years Tom had been in show business. "Forty-one, successfully," he replied. She told him that he had given a lot of people a lot of pleasure.

Sir Tom was accompanied to the palace by his son, daughter and grand-daughter. Dapper and dressed in tails, his new goatee beard proudly jutted from his chin. "Today is just tremendous," he concluded to reporters. "Sometimes you just can't believe it: you think you have been dreaming."

The dream continued. At an age when retirement would be on the minds of most, he was releasing dance hits that were wowing the clubs and planning an extensive winter British tour. He would still, remarkably, be happily doing two hundred shows a year as he drew near to the venerable age of seventy.

One of the most high profile shows of the period had to be the Concert For Diana at Wembley Stadium on 1 July, 2007. The date would have been Diana's 46th birthday. Jones had also that year performed at Hampton Court Palace, but this was a royalty-related event of magnitude, very much in the global spotlight. Tom, of whom the late Princess Diana had been a fan, was joined during his three-song set by Devon soul diva Joss Stone (for 'Ain't That A Lot Of Love') and famed guitar hero Joe Perry of US rock legends Aerosmith. Many raised an eyebrow when Tom, having sung 'Kiss', launched into a version of 'I Bet You Look Good On The Dancefloor', the

RIGHT: Sir Tom can still deliver the sparkle and razzmatazz.

> *Many raised an eyebrow when Tom, having sung 'Kiss',*
> *launched into a version of Arctic Monkeys'*
> *'I Bet You Look Good On The Dancefloor.'*

breakthrough hit from the newly popular Sheffield band Arctic Monkeys.

Hosted by Princes William and Harry (who took a role in booking the acts), the concert was broadcast to an estimated audience of up to 500 million viewers across 140 countries. 63,000 filled the stadium: tickets had sold out the previous December in just 17 minutes. The stellar line-up, mixing established and fast-rising acts, included: Elton John, Duran Duran, Lily Allen, The Feeling, Will Young, Bryan Ferry, Anastasia, Rod Stewart, Kanye West, P. Diddy and Take That. Also appearing were a host of celebrities and comedians from Kiefer Sutherland to David Beckham, from Ricky Gervais to Dennis Hopper. There were pre-recorded messages screened from Bill Clinton, Tony Blair and Nelson Mandela. All net proceeds went to William and Harry's choice of charities.

"The fire is still in me. I don't want to be an oldie, but a goodie. I want to be a contender." In 2008 Tom Jones released his thirty-sixth studio album, *24 Hours*, on S-Curve Records, and undertook a world tour to promote it. It was his first album of new material to get a full American release for a decade and a half. For much of that time he'd been looking to modernise his image by collaborating with or interpreting songs by younger artists from Prince and The Art of Noise to Cerys Matthews

ABOVE: "The fire is still in me."　　　　*OPPOSITE: The hair colour starts to change…*

and Robbie Williams, and triumphantly so. But how it seemed the modern sound around wasn't a million miles away from Tom's own vintage Sixties R&B stylings. With the likes of Mark Ronson and Amy Winehouse bringing polished if processed soul back into fashion, Tom found it easy enough to move with the times by sounding exactly like himself. Full circle!

Aged 68, Tom called on the zeitgeist-y production skills of LA's Future Cut (who'd worked with Lily Allen and Kelis) but knew the blueprints already himself. Producers Nellee Hooper and Betty Wright also chipped in. Tom took a major hand in the song-writing, with help from one or two household names…

Bono and The Edge of U2 provided 'Sugar Daddy' (they also played on it), which seemed intended to come across as a knowing, wry parody of the salacious side of Tom's image. Elsewhere the singer covered Bruce Springsteen's 'The Hitter' and rolled through the old Tommy James hit 'I'm Alive' as a sprightly opening track. The majority of the self-penned material felt poised between light entertainment and confessional soul, but the lyrics offered real, candid glimpses into the man's maturing psyche, as he sent out messages to old friends and family members. There was an element of mea culpa, but with I-did-it-my-way head held high. 'Seasons' cast a rueful eye back over his music career and admitted to mistakes and wrong turns during that water-treading, cabaret-corny middle-phase. 'The Road' went further, big heart on sweaty sleeve. A blue-eyed soul smoulderer, it addresses his wife of half a century Linda. Tom fesses up and apologises to his sometimes errant ways, singing, "I know I caused you pain/I left you shattered on the ground". And he sings it like he means it. Well, it was about time she got a song. He returns to the theme on 'Never', declaring his love for her.

The single "If He Should Ever Leave You", oozing lovelorn sincerity, gained great reviews, with one American magazine, *Spinner*, naming it as one of the best ten songs of the year. After all this time, as the BBC's critic Chris Jones wrote, "The Voice from the Valleys still rings true. At his age, and with a sizeable fortune to fall back on, there's no reason why Jones should even get out of bed. To turn in an album this hungry speaks volumes about his desire to prove that he's still got it. And he has."

Amid the rigours of the world tour he re-emphasised this by performing a rousing 'God Save The Queen' before the Ricky Hatton-Floyd Mayweather Jr. boxing bout and repeated this the next year at Hatton's fight against Manny Pacquiao), and the Welsh national anthem before compatriot Joe Calzaghe's contest with Bernard Hopkins. He was certainly (more than) a contender again. A more

RIGHT: *Mob-bailing is the did't do for...*

glittery and camp promotional activity saw a rendition of 'If He Should Ever Leave You' on *Strictly Come Dancing*. All this must have somehow permeated Hungary, where in 2009 he was voted "sexiest man in the world" by the magazine *Periodika*. At his age!

If Jones was disappointed that *24 Hours* hadn't resulted in any bona fide hit singles, he must have been cheered to find himself at number one again in March 2009, albeit in a comedy offering. His third ever British chart-topping single, 'Islands In The Stream' was a reworking of the Kenny Rogers and Dolly Parton duet written by the peerless Bee Gees brothers. Robin Gibb of that band appeared on the single, as did Rob Brydon and Ruth Jones, Welsh funny-people who'd enjoyed success with the BBC sitcom *Gavin & Stacey*. With the pair of actors referencing that show, the song was released in aid of Comic Relief. While unafraid to poke fun, it simultaneously demonstrated the cast's (and the public's) great affection for the still iconic Mr Jones, who played his part with benign relish. (He and Brydon were to cross paths again.)

One part of the icon did change that year however. Hair-wise, he embraced the grey, giving up on dyeing his hair (and goatee) black. He proudly declared that he'd moved on to a new stage in his life, opting for the silver fox gambit. He told the *Daily Mail*'s Georgina Littlejohn, "I can laugh at myself, but I suddenly thought: it's not the tight trousers they're laughing at now, it's the dyed hair! When my son Mark became my manager, he immediately got me out of the tight trousers and revamped my image. I look back at those trousers and think: Jesus! No wonder!"

This though, had been his own decision. "Over Christmas I always take a month off and don't even shave. Normally it comes out like salt and pepper, which I hated. But this year it grew out a silver colour. So I kept it, because it's more distinguished." The story headline ran pictures under the headline: "Tom Jones, 70, Finally Looks As Old As His 53-Year-Old Son As He Stops Dyeing His Hair". Perhaps managing a showbiz legend who happens to be your dad takes it out of you.

LEFT: Now a fully-fledged 'silver fox'.

6
HYMNS AND VOICES

In 2010, at the age of 70, Tom Jones released an album which again challenged people's perceptions of him and may be his most earthy and stripped-back to date. On 7 June, his birthday, a single – 'Burning Hell', his reading of an old John Lee Hooker classic – emerged, demonstrating a raw, bluesy, no-frills instrumentation and naked vocal with vast emotional heft. *Praise And Blame* went straight into the album charts at number two.

Many critics compared Jones' latest musical move to (the very credible) late Johnny Cash albums, where the country star had gone back to his roots, producer Rick Rubin jettisoning any bells or whistles to expose and highlight the voice. Music site OMH summarised the gambit: "Artists of a certain age hooks up with a name producer to record an album of stripped-down cover versions, leading to both critical acclaim and a whole new audience."

It sure was a long way from 'Sex Bomb' or 'Sugar Daddy'. And the publicity successfully conveyed the impression that Tom was a rebel-artist boldly defying 'the suits' at the record label, going his own way, doing his own fearless thing, sticking it to the man. (And not just a 70-year-old singing hymns). The name producer was Ethan Johns, who had had recent success with Kings of Leon and Paolo Nutini. Guests on the minimalist record included Gillian Welch, Dave Rawlings, Booker T and BJ Cole.

Tom let the music do the talking, but must have felt quietly pleased at its impact and popularity. "It's the first gospel album I've made", he said on a US TV interview. "It's really basic gospel music. It's spiritual music. I used to go to a Presbyterian chapel when I was a boy, and we used to sing hymns on a Sunday afternoon. Then I found out later, when I'd grown up a bit, that a lot of those songs were the same as American gospel music...with a little twist on them. So it's very natural for me."

Although in 2009 Tom had told reporters that he was planning to move back to Britain full-time, after a mere 35 years in the States, he was less certain later. "I've had a great time living in Los Angeles," he said at first, "but after all these years (Linda and I) think now is the time to move home." Yet he was soon refining the view on Chris Moyles' radio show, clarifying that he still lived in LA but visited the UK with increasing frequency. A big Saturday evening TV show was soon to make increasing demands of his time on this side of the pond.

Meanwhile a performance at the Help For Heroes charity concert along with many other stars – at Twickenham Stadium on 11 September, 2010 – enraptured a fifty-thousand strong crowd. Tom sang 'Strange Things Are Happening Every Day' and the perennial 'Green, Green Grass Of Home'. And he was still a welcome guest on major chat shows from Jonathan Ross to David Letterman. A special edition of BBC arts show *Imagine*, entitled 'What Good Am I', was devoted to him, with Alan Yentob conducting interviews with a talkative Tom and fans like Robbie Williams and Cerys Matthews paying homage. Tom was, according to the *Guardian Guide*, "an elemental force with a voice like Thor's own hammer".

Still capable of delivering the unexpected, he popped up on the actor-comedian Hugh Laurie's blues album *Let Them Talk* in May 2011. He helped Laurie promote the record by appearing with him sporadically on television and on stage. He and Laurie sang cuts from the album in New Orleans for a British TV show, *Perspectives*. And his profile was still so high that the final 13 contestants on talent show *American Idol* sang a medley of Tom Jones songs, after which he guested on the show himself.

If Hugh Laurie (though his album proved popular) wasn't the coolest choice of collaborator in the music world, Tom's next musical partner pretty much was. Jack White, once of phenomenally revered garage-blues duo White Stripes and since a solo artist as well as a lynchpin of other critically-acclaimed combos like The Raconteurs and The Dead Weather, found common ground with the Welshman and the pair released a single, blasting out Howlin' Wolf's 'Evil', in March 2012. A must-have cult item, it was made available at first only through independent record shops. The Welsh connection came in

---

PREVIOUS PAGE: The passion is as strong as ever.

OPPOSITE: Older, wiser and still rocking.

when an exclusive three-colour vinyl edition was only sold at one store, Spillers Records in Cardiff. This was the record shop (the oldest in the world, claimed some) where Tom had bought singles as a schoolboy half a century or longer ago. Who said he'd lost touch with his roots? With Jack White being one of the most respected musicians of his generation, the release saw Tom embraced – yet again – by a younger audience.

This was just him limbering up. His next career shift was to prove to be one of the most talked-about in his already hard-to-top history. If talent shows like *The X Factor* and *American Idol* were catnip to some and toxic to others, a new British import wanted to put the music first. Or, more specifically, the singing. Among its pop-tastic panel of judges – or 'coaches' – it required someone with gravitas, with real experience. With the respect of all, across the generations. That's where Tom Jones, the man himself commonly referred to as Jones The Voice – came in.

"Every time I see one of these shows I think half the decisions are wrong and it really frustrates me," said Jones, speaking of shows like The *X Factor*. He was of course promoting new series – and rival to Simon Cowell's dominance – *The Voice*, which began its three-month run in March 2012 and went on to become a much-publicised Saturday night talking point. Tom reckoned the arch enemy failed to discover world-class stars and relied on incompetent judges. "Some of the judges don't have the experience to be on talent shows. If you've only been in the industry two minutes, how can you offer advice? I get fed up – the judging has been questionable. A singing contest should be about someone's voice, not the PR spin." He told *The People*, "I have the experience and I listen to all sorts of music, so the advice I give will be valuable."

For many it was startling that such a legend of five decades at the top had deigned to appear on the panel, but he insisted he felt he could do a better job than the

> *Leonard Cohen's wonderfully world-weary, ironic lyric "I was born with the gift of a golden voice" here testified to the fact that the Welshman always did walk through life with such a gift.*

usual pundits. Another aspect of the show which appealed to him was the Dutch-initiated format, whereby in early rounds – 'blind' auditions – the hopeful singers are chosen or rejected purely on the merits of their voice, with the mentors, backs turned, hearing but not seeing them.

"I'm genuinely excited about *The Voice*," he said. "It's exciting, competitive and compelling television because it's all about talent." He was joined on the 'coaching' staff by the Black Eyed Peas star with the Midas pop touch, will.i.am, ubiquitous new sensation Jessie J, and The Script's vocalist Danny O'Donoghue. In the event it wasn't the *X Factor* but another Cowell-ism, *Britain's Got Talent*, with which *The Voice*, hosted by Holly Willoughby and Reggie Yates, got into a ratings war. The show's winner's prize was £100,000 and a major record deal. "It's all about the voice" became Tom's catchphrase, when he wasn't waxing nostalgic about singing with Elvis and others.

Needless to say, 'Team Tom' provided the winner, seeing off the younger whippersnappers with minimum fuss (though his eyes did well up at the climax). He mentored 28-year-old Leanne Mitchell to victory in the early June final, during which Tom duetted with her on 'Mama Told Me Not To Come'. "Leanne is a fantastic singer and I'm glad her personality is coming out", he beamed. Her debut single, a version of Whitney Houston's 'Run To You', came out the following day, but wasn't a noticeable hit. Indeed the costly show wasn't the runaway ratings success the producers had hoped for. Rumours abound as to whether Tom will return or not for the show's second series, with the *Daily Mail* saying his son Mark was advising him against it. Yet talking to Rob Brydon on his chat show, Tom admitted a few details would need to be ironed out before he committed, then said, "I think I will do another series; we are talking

about it now. One thing I'd need to know is who the other coaches are because I don't want to be sitting there with somebody I don't admire. Hopefully, we will have the same four."

Wasting little time, Tom launched his next project, the top ten album *Spirit In The Room*. Released in May 2012, it echoed the stark, lean sound of its predecessor *Praise And Blame* but ventured into a broader range of material, offering covers of songs from master writers like Leonard Cohen, Paul Simon, Paul McCartney, Tom Waits and Richard and Linda Thompson. Ethan Johns again produced. The *Observer* praised Tom's "enduringly mean set of lungs" as the album swiftly rose to number seven in the charts. Perhaps the highlight was Jones' take on Cohen's 'Tower of Song', a wonderfully world-weary lyric including the famously ironic line, "I was born with the gift of a golden voice," but which here testified to the indisputable fact that the Welshman always did walk through life with such a gift. Some of the song choices were commendably far from obvious – 'I Want To Come Home' isn't McCartney's best-known song (though it became a single for Tom) and 'Love And Blessings' isn't Simon's. In tackling The Low Anthem's 'Charlie Darwin', Jones again showed that he listened to newer artists. Then again, he seemed very at ease on Blind Willie Johnson's 'Soul of a Man'. He let loose manically on Tom Waits' 'Bad As Me' but rendered Richard and Linda Thompson's 'The Dimming of the Day' with weathered elan. BBC reviewer John Aizlewood pointed out how comfortable in his own skin Jones now sounded, suggesting that *Spirit In The Room* was "if anything, even more pared down, even more emotionally adult and rueful" than *Praise And Blame*. Between them the two albums reinvented him as "a God-fearing, fundamentally flawed man coming to terms with his own mortality."

OPPOSITE: Tom rocks Britannia at the The Queen's Diamond Jubilee Concert.

NEXT PAGES: Sir Tom proves that you can age gracefully and still be cool.

Jones himself said, "It was about making it as authentic as possible, and not trying to flower it up too much". Speaking about the Leonard Cohen track, he said to OMH, "If I could write like that I would. You know – 'my hair is gray, I ache in the places where I used to play…' And as for 'I was born like this…" – I had no choice, really, I've got this voice, this is the road I had to take! I read that and thought: I've got to do it."

An interview with Rob Brydon to promote the album led to the comedian spoofing Sir Tom's persistent cough on chat shows with the singer looking benignly on, a twinkle in his eye. The same twinkle glinted as he performed at the Queen's Diamond Jubilee Concert outside Buckingham Palace. "I've always been a royalist. Holding on to the royal family the way the British people have is a wonderful thing, and it shows in America especially: it's something they don't have." By September he was playing Hyde Park at a big Radio 2 show and then, for BBC4, a more intimate show at the LSO St Luke's. *GQ*, in its Men of the Year issue, declared him a "legend", writing, "If Frank Sinatra was an American icon because he was the guy who had it all, lost it all, and got it all back again, then the 72-year-old Welshman is our national treasure because he's got it all back again more times than anyone can remember, including probably himself."

Earlier in his incomparable career, Sir Tom had said, "Only the public can decide how big you are. If the public stopped coming to see me, I'd be in trouble." It seems very unlikely that that will ever now happen. Interviewed in the *Guardian* recently, Tom mused that his most treasured possession is "my voice", his favourite smell is "the scent of a woman" and that his fantasy dinner party guests would be Winston Churchill, John Wayne and Boudicca. His greatest achievement was his knighthood and he'd like to be remembered as "a helluva singer". Asked what his choice of super-power would be, he answered, "Immortality".

Given the way Tom Jones has lived his life and sung his songs so far, it'd be something of a risk to rule that out.

" *I had no choice, really: This is the road I had to remembered as a helluva*

I've got this voice.
take! I'd like to be
singer. "

INDEX

CREDITS

The publishers would like to thank the following sources for their kind permission to reproduce the pictures in this book

2. Mirrorpix, 6. Rex Features/Simon Dack, 9. Getty Images/Harry Langdon, 10. Alamy/Pictorial Press Ltd, 11. Getty Images/Carsten Windhorst/Photoshot, 12-13. Mirrorpix, 14 & 15. Alamy/Pictorial Press Ltd, 17. Corbis/Hulton-Deutsch Collection, 18 & 21. Mirrorpix, 22-23. Getty Images/ABC Photo Archives, 25. Press Association Images, 26-27. Rex Features/ITV, 28. Getty Images/Popperfoto, 29. Getty Images/Ian Tyas/Keystone Features, 30-31. Rex Features/Daily Sketch, 32. Getty Images/ABC Photo Archives, 33. Corbis/Pierre Fournier/Sygma, 34. Mirrorpix, 35. Getty Images/ABC Photo Archives, 36. Getty Images/Terry O'Neill (top), Press Association Images (bottom), 36-37. Getty Images/ Chris Ware/Keystone Features, 38. Rex Features/Dave Magnus, 39. Corbis/ Pierre Fournier/Sygma, 40. Mirrorpix (top & bottom), 40-41. Corbis/ Bettmann, 42. Alamy/Keystone Pictures USA, 43. Rex Features/Harold Gold, 44. Getty Images/CBS Photo Archive, 45. Getty Images/Terry Disney/Express, 46. Getty Images/Paul Popper/Popperfoto, 47. Corbis/ Hulton-Deutsch Collection (left), Getty Images/Terry O'Neill (right), 48-49 Corbis/Tony Frank/Sygma, 50-51 Corbis/Sygma, 52. Alamy/Pictorial Press Ltd, 53. Rex Features, 54. Getty Images/Michael Ochs Archives, 55. Alamy/Keystone Pictures USA, 56. Press Association Images, 57. Getty Images/Popperfoto, 58. Getty Images/Bentley Archive/Popperfoto, 59. Corbis/Pierre Fournier/Sygma, 60. Corbis/Tony Frank/Sygma, 61. Alamy/ Pictorial Press Ltd, 62-63. Getty Images/Jan Persson/Redferns, 66-67. Getty Images/Michael Ochs Archives, 69. Getty Images/ABC Photo Archives, 70. Getty Images/Terry O'Neill, 71. Getty Images/David Corio/ Redferns, 72. Alamy/Keystone Pictures USA, 73, 74 & 75. Getty Images/ Terry O'Neill, 76. Getty Images/ABC Photo Archives, 77. Getty Images/ GAB/Redferns, 78-79, Getty Images/ABC Photo Archives, 80. Mirrorpix, 81. Getty Images/Terry O'Neill, 82. Getty Images/Richard Patrick/AFP, 83 & 84. Mirrorpix x2, 85 & 86-87. Getty Images/ABC Photo Archives, 88. Mirrorpix x2, 88-89. Getty Images/Richard Melloul/Sygma, 90. Rex Features (left), Rex Features/Valley Music Ltd, 91. Mirrorpix, 92-93. Rex Features/Valley Music Ltd, 94. Getty Images/Harry Langdon, 96-97. Rex Features/Associated Newspapers, 98. Getty Images/Bob King/Redferns, 101. Mirrorpix, 103. Getty Images/Rico D'Rozario/Redferns, 104. Getty Images/Tim Roney/Hulton Archive, 106-107. Getty Images/Bernd Mueller/Redferns, 108. Mirrorpix, 109. Getty Images/Joseph Del Valle/ NBCU Photo Bank, 110. Rex Features/Steve Wood, 111. Corbis/Lynn Goldsmith, 113. Corbis/Rob Brown, 114-115. Rex Features/Moviestore Collection, 116. Corbis/Gary Moss, 117. Getty Images/Mick Hutson/ Redferns, 120-121. Press Association Images, 123. Rex Features/Richard Young, 124. Getty Images/Nicky J. Sims/Redferns, 125. Getty Images/ Ron Galella, WireImage, 126. Rex Features, 127. Corbis/Chris Farina, 129. Contour by Getty Images/Smallz & Raskind, 130-131. Mirrorpix, 132. Getty Images/David Tonge, 133. Corbis/Dana Lixenberg, 134-135. Getty Images/Patrick Ford/Redferns, 136-137. Getty Images/Dave Hogan, 138. Rex Features/Andy Paradise, 139. Rex Features/Brian Rasic, 140-141. Rex Features/Ray Tang, 142-143. Getty Images/Photoshot, 144-145. Corbis/ Rune Hellestad, 147. Corbis/Simone Cecchetti, 148. Getty Images/Jim Dyson, 149. Getty Images/Ben Pruchnie, 150. Getty Images/ABC Photo Archive, 151 & 152. Getty Images/Dave Hogan, 154-155 & 160. Mirrorpix